Raising the Bar
Creating and Nurturing Adaptability to
Deal with the Changing Face of War

Don Vandergriff

Dedicated to those who carry the burden of freedom: Soldiers

TABLE OF CONTENTS

Introduction

"Adaptability" has become a buzzword throughout the U.S. Army due to experiences in Afghanistan and Iraq. This is the Army's introduction to 4th generation warfare. The Army recognizes that in order to move toward becoming a "learning organization" where leaders practice adaptability, it will have to change its culture, particularly its leader development paradigm. The challenge is great, but signs are beginning to appear that it might be possible as new ideas are implemented.

Today's leader development paradigm evolved from one that worked to support the nation's long-standing mobilization doctrine. Mobilization doctrine relies on a small core of full time professional soldiers, backed by large militias or National Guard forces in peacetime, to be prepared to expand rapidly in the event of a national emergency – such as war. Successful mobilization requires time and massive resources. Time is needed to get troops prepared, while resources compensate for lack of experience, professionalism and cohesion needed to fight and win a war.

To support the mobilization doctrine, the Army developed leadership training methods that paralleled management training practices in the corporate structures of the Industrial Age. The challenge for the Army was to get millions of citizens with little or no military experience and turn them into soldiers and officers in a short time. Industry provided the answers, and in the aftermath of the glow of victory in several wars, these approaches became institutionalized. Some modifications were applied to leader development, but they happened along the fringes of existing laws, regulations, policies and beliefs.

Army alterations to today's leader development paradigm may not be enough. The Army has "thought" and "acted" from an antiquated, mobilization-based leader development paradigm that still exists more than 16 years after the fall of the Berlin Wall. This Industrial Age model continues to shape the way the Army approaches its training and education, often defining both as one. Consequently, the Army's leader development paradigm – designed for an earlier era – has been so intimately tied to the maintenance of current Army culture that a self-perpetuating cycle has formed that diminishes and even prevents the Army from developing adaptive leaders and institutions. This cycle can only be broken if the Army accepts rapid evolutionary change as the norm of the new era.

Cultural change begins with the application of a new leader development model in place of techniques being used today in both institutions and operational units. A new leader development approach known as the Adaptive Course Model (ACM) is cultural rather than a prescribed list of procedures and exercises. ACM develops adaptability through the use of outstanding teachers who use the experiential learning model to teach the Rapid Decision-Making (RDM) process. ACM forms the beginning of the next revolution – a revolution in education – that will spur an evolution into a new personnel management system centered on professionalism and flexibility. This book will focus on how to begin the evolution into a new leader paradigm.

So I respond to the warning of Army Chief of Staff Gen. Peter Schoomaker in an e-mail to me in November 2004, "...we have lots to do," with the belief that cultural change is generational and begins with how the Army develops its future leaders.[1]

Preface

Raising the Bar: Creating and Nurturing Adaptability to Deal with the Changing Face of War began as a study in the winter of 2004 and spring of 2005 on how to create adaptive leaders and holistically reform the Army Reserve Officer Training Corps (ROTC). More importantly, it was the beginning of a comprehensive effort to reform the leadership paradigm of the Army.[2] However, while the original study focused on the Army's ROTC, this monograph seeks to address the Army's approach to leader development and in particular its methods of teaching and nurturing adaptability.

The purpose of this monograph is threefold. First, it will briefly outline the need to change the Army leader development paradigm, created and sustained for its 100-year-old mobilization doctrine. Second, the monograph will state what the Army needs to develop these leaders, the requisite monolithic capabilities and competencies. Third, it will describe and propose a new professional leader educational model that the Army must develop that is neither "training" nor "education" in the conventional sense, but rather something in between, and focuses on "how" rather than "what" to think.[3]

The study has several target audiences. First and foremost, this monograph is directed toward Army senior leaders who are in a position to adjust specific teaching methods and prepare young leaders for the evolution of war. Second, this study hopes to reach the instructional cadre at Army organizations located throughout the country tasked with leader and decision-making development. Finally, this monograph endeavors to present the general public – anyone interested in leader development – with an assortment of ideas outside of the scope of their ongoing efforts, and to provide teachers with a "lessons-learned" or "best-practices" document. Most importantly, the public must understand that reform to prepare for the future is about leadership and people.

As such, the monograph also provides lessons and insights on teaching leadership and adaptability in a generic sense and, therefore, has important lessons beyond the Army, such as in business and politics.

The author's professional experiences, research and interaction with fellow military professionals suggest that a cultural revolution within the U.S. military is essential if the nation is to successfully adapt and prevail in the emerging 4th generation warfare (4GW) or asymmetric warfare threat environment.

An Army cultural revolution has three parts:

1. Strategic leaders must change a counterproductive array of long-established beliefs including many laws, regulations and policies, which are based on out-of-date assumptions.

2. Military leaders must drive and sustain a military cultural evolution through effective education and training of the next generation(s) of leaders in a system that is flexible enough to evolve alongside emerging changes in, and lessons from, war, society and technology.

3. Finally, senior leaders must continue to nurture and protect these younger leaders as they go out and put to practice what they have learned, and allow them to evolve.

When the Army begins and sustains an evolutionary process of cultural change based on these or similar principles, it will be on the road to effective reform. This study aims to provide ways to plot and follow the transformational road map for the Army and nation to deal with the complexities of 4th generation warfare.

Donald E. Vandergriff
Woodbridge, Va.

Prologue

"I've thought for years the Army needed to transform its personnel system, and change the way that we develop leaders."

Gen. Peter Schoomaker, Army Chief of Staff

"Changing and Fighting, Simultaneously" *Government Executive Magazine*, Oct. 23, 2004

Why does Army leadership development need to be transformed? The nature of warfare has not changed, but the methods and conduct of fighting wars are shifting dramatically. A new vision of "future" warfare first appeared in a 1989 *Marine Corps Gazette* article entitled, "The Changing Face of War: Into the fourth generation," written by William S. Lind, Marine Corps Reserve Lt. Col. G.I. Wilson, Army Lt. Col. Joseph W. Sutten, and Marine Corps Capt. John F. Schmidt. The article reflected on the U.S. Army and Marine Corps war-fighting doctrine of the past and how training, education and acquisition has always been centered on large, identifiable foes with professional standing armies.

In contrast, modern warfare, coined by the authors as "4th generation warfare" (4GW) requires the military to reorient toward a new kind of threat – unidentifiable, disparate groups rather than state-sponsored armies – i.e. the U.S. opponents in the ongoing war in Iraq. An examination of 4GW theory provides valuable insight into how the U.S. Army should examine and shape its current leadership development paradigm. In other words, a new enemy requires new leaders.

For the purposes of this monograph, the term 1st generation warfare (1GW) refers to the era of state warfare, close-quarters fighting before the age of Napoleon. Second generation warfare (2GW), also known as Industrial Age or attrition warfare, grew out of the French Revolution. 2GW is state-versus-state warfare characterized by the emphasis on mobilizing resources, and fighting centrally controlled armies.

In contrast, 3rd generation (3GW) conflicts evolved from the German attempts during World War I to break the trench stalemate on the Western Front by using ideas instead of technology; this prompted the use of decentralized tactics moving toward a common goal. Between World War I and II, the Germans moved what they had done from the tactical to the operational level of war. The emphasis on 3GW was on speed, forcing the enemy to always react to multiple and rapid actions.

The cultures that define 2GW and 3GW are also different. Generally the former is a top-down, centralized, bureaucratic hierarchy, where information flows up while decisions go down, and there is little trust. 3GW, on the other hand, is a culture that demands and depends on high levels of trust based on high levels of professionalism in order to create the decentralized decision-making that is a step ahead of its opponents.

Finally, 4th generation warfare has emerged, of which insurgency is just one aspect. It is non-state warfare, where organizations with no loyalty to the centralized power of a state, can and do wage wars with the state or other non-state organizations. The rise of affordable and available off-the-shelf technology enables 4GW opponents, using small yet highly trained groups, to take on larger and more powerful state armies. The goal of a 4GW opponent is to defeat the mind and destroy the cohesion of the opponent's decision-makers through any means possible.

Fourth generation warfare will not replace 2GW and 3GW conflict, but will co-exist alongside it. As the state system continues to weaken, however, it will be the warfare of choice for non-state organizations that wish to confront state militaries trained and equipped for the earlier generations.

To counter the new enemy and potential future threats, the Army is enduring one of the greatest transformations since the reforms made under Secretary of War Elihu Root at the beginning of the 20th century. Army reform has been dominated by tangibles that can be measured such as weapons, force structure, and doctrine. These aspects receive most of the attention during periods of reform, from decision-makers both in and out of uniform.

Fortunately, it appears that for the first time in its history, the Army is beginning to address its training deficiencies and act to change its leader development paradigm. Though it faces major obstacles to carry through with its plans, at the heart of any organization are its leaders. It will take leaders to change the culture.

"Leadership" is an intangible concept that is hard to measure; leaders are often criticized but good leadership can be difficult to implement. However, if the necessary changes discussed in this study are tested, it will provide an invaluable advantage for the Army and the nation in dealing with evolving and dangerous enemies.

By adopting a new leader paradigm, in tandem with other complicated tasks such as modularity – how the Army organizes its forces for a particular mission – and the Future Combat System (FCS), the Army has embarked upon in its transformation, a necessary first step. To move from a mobilization-based Army, geared for conventional conflict against a "peer competitor" like the Soviet Union, to a future "Army with expeditionary and joint capabilities" for unconventional conflict against a range of adversaries, requires an evolution in Army culture.

Why is that so? Why is it easy to say the Army is going to create "adaptive leaders" during a Power Point presentation, but so difficult to put those words into action? Understanding leadership and how to develop leaders to be adaptive, and subsequently how to nurture those traits with the right command environment and organizational culture, is very hard. It requires current leaders at all levels to have a shared vision of change, and a thorough understanding of U.S. military and civilian history as both have evolved with the nation's experiences in war.

Leaders advocating change must understand the "why" and "how" to effectively reform the method the Army uses to develop adaptive leaders. Current leaders must be able to communicate why change is necessary in terms that everyone else understands – perhaps the hardest thing to do given the rhetoric of the last 20 years on how great the Army and its institutions have been in preparing leaders and soldiers for war. The Army has done a good job in preparing leaders for war but in the context of 2GW and 3GW.[4]

The Army is beginning to do a better job preparing its leaders for the future. But how far will it go to prepare them for 4GW? The Army also needs a cultural revolution beginning with changes in leader education. This effort must be dramatic and much larger than the training revolution led by Gen. Paul Gorman, and the education revolution led by then Lt. Col. Huba Wass de Czege when he established the Army's elite School of Advanced Military Studies known as SAMS in 1983. Both occurred in the aftermath of Vietnam to prepare the Army for high intensity conflict against the Soviet Union, but in support of the mobilization doctrine.

SAMS became the second year of the Army's Command and General Staff College (C&GSC). Only a select few attended this additional year to study large unit operations and grasp an understanding of the operational level of war. It was a shock to an institution and profession whose focus was fixed on the tactical level of war presented through a Program of Instruction (POI) that had changed little in format since the founding of C&GSC in the late 1800s.[5]

The new education revolution will require more than glaring words on briefing slides, or changing the names, but not the substance, of current leader-centric courses (this includes non-commissioned officers, civilians as well as the development that occurs in operational units).

The current approach to leadership training (development) is similar to Sir Isaac Newton's view of the world, which has become the Army's view. Newton's world view defines war as linear and easy to measure with numbers.[6] As John Schmidt described in Command and (Out of) Control: The Military Implications of Complexity Theory, when applying the complexity theory to war:[7]

The great Prussian military theorist-philosopher Carl von Clausewitz was an avid amateur scientist who relied heavily and explicitly on the physical sciences to provide metaphors for his military concepts. Two of his greatest and most enduring concepts – friction and the center of gravity – come straight out of the science of the day. Of course, science for Clausewitz was a Newtonian science. The Newtonian paradigm is the mechanistic paradigm: the world and everything in it as a giant machine. The preferred Newtonian metaphor is the clock, consisting of finely tooled gears meshing smoothly and precisely, ticking along predictably, measurably and reliably, keeping perfect time.[8]

Root of the culture

Today's Army culture began its cultural evolution toward linearity and the Newtonian way of war alongside the emergence of the large corporations and industrial captains of the late 1800s. They embraced the theories and practices of Frederick Taylor (1856-1915), the great managerial and labor industrial theorist of the late 1800s and early 1900s. Taylor was explicit about his intentions to use "scientific management" to control capitalist means and conditions of production.[9]

Later, these methods evolved into the Lanchesterian models, which were scientific tools of trend analysis, determination and sample means used to predict the outcome of battles. In the Army this is referred to as "the arithmetic of the battlefield" or "battlefield math." The "Lanchester" equations modeled the outcome of battles as a function of force ratios, focusing on losses and the attrition of forces only. In turn, this told the Army personnel system what type and how many "parts" it would need.[10]

Root's reforms further evolved the recommendations of U.S. Army Maj. Gen. Emory Upton (1839-1881), the leading reformer in trying to move the Army from the frontier to full time professionalism based on the Prussian model. Nonetheless, Root's interpretation of Upton's work (he died before Root took office) followed the preaching of Taylor.[11] As a result, Root's reforms moved the U.S. Army from a constabulary force, reliant on an undependable militia system, to a force that could fight in a major war with and against the armies of European nation-states. Finally, these reforms also took into account the primacy of the individual that remains at the heart of the U.S. Constitution. Root's new system could not appear to threaten American democracy by postulating a military that was separate and isolated from civilian society. Root combined the popular corporate management practices of Taylor with the emerging theories of personnel management in the Progressive Era. Root's system promised individualism because it appeared to give everyone a "level playing field" in which to move up to the top.

For the Army, Root's reforms provided the beginning of a culture that could support the distinctive mobilization doctrine of the United States. It was a doctrine that worked well as long as the United States was fighting a linear war.[12] However the U.S. Army today, and for the near future, is not fighting linear wars.

The critical aspect of Root's reforms involved personnel management initiatives that rode the wave of scientific management then sweeping the nation and the Western world. At the time Root first implemented these measures, any adjustments brought improvements to the bedraggled post-Civil War Army. However, what began as reform soon became a bureaucratic straitjacket that would have long-lasting, negative impacts on later generations of officers, enlisted soldiers and the Army as an institution.

Ironically, policies that favored the primacy of the individual alongside institutional rhetoric of selfless service created a culture of conflict that few, if any, could escape.[13] These laws and supporting policies have become legacies, or "untouchables" that the Army culture sees as necessary to its very function. The legacies support an increasing motivation of individuals fueled by self-interest that pits the espoused selflessness of Army values, especially among leaders, against careerism.

Success on the battlefield against opponents as weak as the Iraqi conventional army in 1991 and 2003 has made it harder to recognize and cure the entrenched flaws in Army culture. The "glow of victory" after each war has allowed the nation's political and military leadership to ignore important "lessons learned" – especially negative ones.

"Lessons learned" in the first Iraq war could have been applied to improving the Army and its leaders to fight the next, much more difficult war that began in Iraq after the fall of Baghdad in April 2003.[14] But this did not happen. Therefore, badly needed reforms to Army personnel laws and shifts in the service's cultural beliefs – which defined in large part how officers had been created, trained and educated for future war – were the first casualties of the easy victories in 1991 and 2003. Far too many leaders saw victory, and a lack of an immediate post-Cold War threat, as validation for the old ways of doing things, and used those examples to defeat any attempts at effective reform.[15]

If the Army is in fact going to "transform" itself, sustaining and enhancing that change will be impossible without also transforming how the Army creates its next generation of leaders. The service will have to move from its century-old heritage of linear training to an educational system that creates and sustains adaptability to deal with the complexity of modern war. This would be a major paradigm shift.

The obstacles to change also include the American public's longtime resistance to the professionalization of the officer corps. The prevailing attitude among educational leaders and academics in the nation's colleges and universities has been that the military academies were "bastions of aristocracy" and that their graduates in the officer corps were "isolated from their civilian contemporaries."[16]

The American public has long accepted this concept, and thus supported the Reserve Officer Training Corps (ROTC) and other officer training programs as a counter-balance to the cadre of professional officers coming out of U.S. military academies.

As a result, any move within the Army to evolve leadership development programs that include professional entrance portals within traditional fields such as law, medicine or engineering would spark resistance from the general public as being too militaristic or, in a cultural sense, too "European." Surprisingly, despite the threats the United States faces today, this entrenched attitude remains an invisible barrier to reforming how the Army develops leaders for the 21st century.[17]

To reshape the U.S. military, particularly the Army, into a force that can be successful at prosecuting future, non-linear wars requires something unprecedented in American military history: a culture of innovation.

Culture of innovation

The good news is that there are situations where U.S. Army leaders have been adaptive and innovative in a 4GW conflict. One example arising from the wars in Iraq and Afghanistan is Lt. Col. Chris Hughes (now Colonel), a battalion commander in the 101st Airborne Division (Air Assault), who found his unit faced by an angry mob in Nasiriyah in April 2003 during the U.S.-led invasion of Iraq. His response was to order his soldiers to take off their sunglasses, kneel down and smile. That simple yet totally unconventional (by the Army book) ploy worked!

A totally un-military, yet innovative, approach enabled Hughes, his unit, the Army and the United States to retain the "moral high ground" in that one small corner of Iraq. Over time, Hughes and his unit set the example for the entire division on how to successfully fight a 4GW by not fighting, and by taking steps to understand the local culture.[18] There is the potential to create many more leaders like Hughes by addressing today's leader development paradigm.

The leader development paradigm includes how leaders are initially selected and assessed, educated and trained, as well as promoted and selected for key positions. All of these institutions under the leader development paradigm must work in harmony to produce and nurture the qualities that made Hughes successful in a complicated environment. Otherwise, the nation and the Army will only find cases of innovation as an exception to the rule.[19]

As Brig. Gen. David Fastabend and Robert Simpson define in the article "Adapt or Die":

A culture of innovation is typified by an environment within which every single person in the organization is invested in the organization's success and feels a responsibility to implement new and better ways to achieve organizational objectives. People are encouraged to try alternative paths, test ideas to the point of failure, and learn from the experience. Experimentation and prudent risk-taking are admired and encouraged. Experimentation is not a destination to be reached, but an unending process of trial, feedback, learning, renewal and experimentation again.

The organization as a whole is agile, ready to learn, continually changing and improving. It is fast, flexible and never prepared to say: "We have finished getting better." Innovative organizations depend less on forecasting, planning and control and more on scanning, agility and feedback. Innovative organizations embrace uncertainty, recognizing that an uncertain future potentially holds as many opportunities as it does threats.[20]

The Army must reshape its educational institutions and training programs for leadership development into what Fastabend and Simpson identified as a "Learning Organization."[21] This is broadly defined as an organization that can evolve with its operating environment by rapid application of lessons learned. Such organizations can deal with complexity and uncertainty in war because people at all levels are capable of proactively developing and implementing new ways of achieving individual, unit, and institutional excellence and effectiveness.

This manuscript offers specific structural and procedural reforms to today's Army leader development paradigm that the author has concluded has been left behind by the Information Age. Currently, the core system by which the Army recruits and trains its future officers is ill-equipped to provide a cadre of future adaptive leaders.

Beyond technology

At present, reforming the U.S. military education system is a hot topic within the overall discussion of transforming the military to better deal with the changing face of war – specifically 4GW (though to date the military does not accept the term 4GW, and instead calls it asymmetric warfare). It's not a mystery, given the sudden appetite for analysis on the topic by retired military leaders, think tanks, defense consultants and TV show "talking heads," that this subject has taken off. U.S. commanders – at all levels – and junior officers and non-commissioned officers in the field in Afghanistan and Iraq are facing new and complex problems that are forcing even the traditionalists and ardent technocrats to confront the human factors and intangibles of 4GW.

Experience on the ground is providing undeniable proof that there are problems with the existing Army system for developing leaders who must adapt to significantly changing conditions.[22] With some exceptions, leaders deployed to Iraq and Afghanistan were prepared for 2GW and 3GW, but not for 4GW that arose after the capture of Baghdad in April 2003. Apart from the preparation of Special Forces leaders and some exceptional individual units, the Army's education and training systems did not go far enough to prepare leaders to deal with the chaotic situations they found in the 4GW world.

Lt. Col. Jim Chevallier, commander of 1st Squadron, 4th Cavalry said that his leaders and soldiers were prepared for 2GW, but were unprepared for the 4GW environment:

I don't think we came in with leaders fully prepared to fight counterinsurgency... an understanding of our enemy and how he operates. We did a very good job in training specific TTPs [tactics, techniques and procedures], such as how to react to an IED [improvised explosive device], but I don't think we understood what our enemy's basic scheme of maneuver was. For example, you go three to five days when it's IEDs, and that's all you find – then three to five days when it's attacks on the ISF [Iraqi security force] – it was our ability to understand and counter that. I think it's important for leaders to read and understand the classics on counterinsurgency so they can define for their soldiers what success is in this environment. For example, there's an attack from an orchard – there are several techniques I could use to counter that. One is to bulldoze the orchard, but in doing so I just create more insurgents. So, until you understand counterinsurgency, it's difficult to tell what success is. If I had to do it all over again, I'd train my leaders more on counterinsurgency operations.[23]

The Army's 2GW linear system left Army leaders, especially junior officers, not as prepared to adapt to the unexpected demands of the ongoing wars in Afghanistan and Iraq. While one should applaud the fact that some leaders were able to adapt, the question remains why were many not?

As a corollary, how did those who did not adapt impact the ability of campaigns to succeed in both Afghanistan and Iraq? At the writing of this manuscript, the significant negative impact of not adapting in the first year of the occupation of Iraq war was only beginning to become apparent, despite the ongoing Herculean efforts of most leaders and soldiers to accomplish the mission.[24]

More critical are the strategic consequences of this inability to adapt. As one captain reported, "The bottom line is that you can have 99 captains who adapted, but it is the one that does not who can ruin everything the others accomplished."[25] Thus, there is a flurry of activity today as think tanks and military task forces propose various changes to military education, from mid-level officer career courses to senior-level war college programs.[26]

After long study and analysis of the Army's existing system, it is clear that focusing efforts on people who already have had their character defined and shaped by the antiquated personnel system, or what I refer to as today's leader paradigm, will be ineffective. Rather, the effective transformation of the Army requires the cultivation of a very different military mindset, starting at the cadet, or pre-commissioning, level. As one former ROTC cadet – now a captain serving with Special Forces – recently observed: "Why not begin the reform where it all begins?"

Reform efforts, the captain correctly argues, should start with the next generation of potential leaders: earlier is better. This means that reforms to leadership development will begin a cultural evolution that ultimately will transform the Army as a whole.[27] Changing the culture of the Army and the military is generational and begins with the Army's newest and potential leaders.

The question of the financial and political costs of such sweeping reform will be asked from the outset, but what will be the cost to the nation if we don't change our current military system? Even the most cursory glance at the Pentagon's current budget growth will underscore the fact that the nation cannot afford to simply throw more money at the problem.

In addition to the billions of dollars in outlays to the campaigns in Iraq and Afghanistan, the time is approaching when the federal government will be confronted by the requirement to pay massive Social Security and Medicare outlays for the retiring baby-boom generation.

Thus, the real question is: How much longer can the United States continue to afford ever-increasing defense budgets to pay for highly complex and expensive weapons systems that are designed for the wrong kind of conflict – linear warfare?[28] In other words, the money would be better spent on improving human training than expensive weapons systems that do not properly address the needs for 4GW warfare.

Addressing these budget pressures along with transforming the Army to enable it to successfully fight and survive in a new form of warfare begins with changing the culture. To effect culture change, one must inspect the existing system for educating future leaders and critically analyze all aspects beginning with: What was the system established to do? What type of doctrine did it support? And finally, what type of enemies did it expect its leaders to fight?

Linearity meets complexity

What is wrong with the current military culture? The answer lies in a question: Is the current approach to officer development, which has evolved from theories, practices and cultural beliefs over a hundred years, the right one for the future?[29] Simply put, it is not. While the current system has provided a model for leader development and has sufficed for the nation's conventional warfare mobilization doctrine, it is not suited for expeditionary, "come as you are," warfare that characterizes 4GW. Most of the problems stem from the fact that the systems in place today are "legacy systems" that were developed for an era and form of warfare that have been overcome by events.[30]

The Army's traditional mindset that manifests itself in culture, rather than technology, appears to be the major obstacle to evolving adaptability, not only in its members, but also in its institutions. Without question, the Army has the technology and the type of people to decentralize control and increase discretion downward to the front lines of action and throughout the organization. Nevertheless, the Army must evolve its culture to meet the expectations of those leaders that adapt in both combat and in its institutions, instead of expecting them to conform to the past bureaucratic mindset, and thus, lose their most valuable asset – people.[31]

A recurring problem is that the Army keeps trying to reform the unalterable, attempting to improve something that cannot be improved because it was developed for a different time. While many well-intentioned people are trying to succeed in changing the current culture by making only incremental adjustments to existing personnel and educational systems, the Army must be willing to literally practice what it preaches when it says it wants to become a "learning organization."[32]

The complexity of 21st century warfare demands something new and different – and something that will work. Conventional linear thinking cannot cope with tomorrow's non-linear challenges: enter complexity theory.

Three informative books – Chaos, Making a New Science, by James Gleick; Complexity: The Emerging Science at the Edge of Order and Chaos, by Mitchell Waldrop; and Hidden Order: How Adaptation Builds Complexity, by John Holland – provide an answer for how the Army could embrace non-linear complexity theory to change both its leadership development paradigm and its culture to meet 21st century warfare.

Briefly put, complexity theory postulates how complex systems are capable of generating simple patterns, and conversely, how simple systems are capable of displaying complex behaviors.

An American military strategist who is increasingly being recognized for his thinking on such issues, the late Air Force Col. John Boyd, recognized that land warfare has much in common with complex systems, while complex, adaptive systems – where small initial changes can produce significantly larger outcomes – have much in common with 4th generation warfare.[33] Why is complexity theory better suited for 4th generation warfare?

Foundation

Before complexity theory emerged as an inspiration for organizational paradigms, the Army followed the corporate world example, structuring its activities in a framework based on Frederick Taylor's theories of managing and training workers as discussed earlier. Taylor's theories were influenced by Newtonian determinism, which applies linear thinking to the development of leaders.[34]

Taylor's greatest contribution to production efficiency was to break down complex production tasks into a sequence of simple, standardized steps. This permitted him to design a standardized mass production line around a management system that classified work into standard tasks and workers into standard specialties. This combination established work standards and the people who were trained to these standards became interchangeable cogs in the machine. This greatly simplified personnel management in a vast industrial enterprise.

To be sure, Taylorism transformed industrial production, but it also had a dark side: Taylorism treated people as unthinking cogs in a machine. By necessity, these people had to accept a social system based on a coercive pattern of dominance and subordination and centralized control from the top. Every action and every decision made in the organization was spelled out in the name of efficiency. In theory, the entire regimen flowed from the brain of one individual at the top of the hierarchy.

A complimentary management dogma also emerged during the Progressive Era. This was the theory of "ethical egoism," which asserted that all people are motivated solely by self-interest. By extension, all people would respond predictably to a variety of positive incentives (money, pleasure, advancement, distinction, power, luxurious prestige goods, and amenities) or negative incentives (which took the primary form of a fear of losing the positive benefits, but also outright punishment and pain).

The two previous modern phenomena were laid on top of the final factor that had already existed during the Industrial Age as the education philosophy of René Descartes. Descartes was a famous mathematician who broke down engineering problems in sequence, making it easier to teach formulas to engineering students. This approach was translated into French military training, where the French found it easy to break down military problem solving into processes (checklists) to educate their officers and their awaiting masses of citizen soldiers upon mobilization. This approach was in turn copied by the U.S. Army as a way to turn mobilized citizens into soldiers and leaders quickly.[35]

The Cartesian approach allowed the French (and later the United States) to easily teach a common, fundamental doctrinal language to many who were new to the military. It significantly reduced the time it took to master basic military skills. The downfall of this approach is that it simplifies war (complex problems) into processes where the enemy is only a template, not a free-thinking adversary.

The Cartesian approach also slows down a decision cycle by turning the planners' focus inward, on process, instead of outward on the enemy. The problem with this approach is that it's hard to adapt to whatever problems are at hand. It is the same thing with operations research, which is a powerful tool, but only for solving certain well-defined problems.

The problem with the U.S. military is that it applies a mechanical approach to all sorts of inappropriate problems including leader development, specifically education. The French, and then the United States, while relying on a massed citizen army in the late 19th and early 20th centuries, had to find a way to instruct many citizen officers quickly in military doctrine. Additionally, because of the casualties of World War I and the advance of modern weaponry and its destructiveness, the French needed a way to teach its officers how to control these resources to concentrate firepower so they could compensate for their lack of unit skills on the battlefields. They used an orderly and systematic approach to planning that was similar to the Military Decision-Making Process (MDMP).[36]

When the new U.S. Army arrived in Europe in 1917, it was led largely by citizens who had been transformed into officers almost overnight, and its soldiers needed to learn the fundamentals of the profession of arms quickly. All U.S. staff officers and commanders attended French schools in planning and controlling forces in combat. The United States and France were the victors in World War I and saw that victory as a validation of their training process. When the French developed methodical battle in the interwar years, the United States copied it with all its accompanying process-focused education. The U.S. Army carried this over to its education and training, as well as its doctrine.[37]

France and the United States practiced Progressive Era personnel theories and opened the net wide to accessions in order to be democratic and fair. Missing from this practice was a hard "filter" to judge character under stress prior to awarding a commission. It was felt that new officers could learn on the job either in peacetime duty or in war. This was a very harsh way to develop and prepare leaders. Both countries felt that they were the victors in war without examining why they were the victors, and they ignored mistakes and lessons learned.

In sum, the combination of policies and beliefs that Descartes, Taylor and Root began in the Progressive Era are seen today through easier accessions, faster promotions, no obligation to attend essential leader training school, the refusal to allow cadre to kick out non-performers, and quicker pay raises. These policies are fully consistent with their theory of human behavior and they stem from the idea that a system has a need to fill spaces with faces.

Taken together, the idea that people are interchangeable cogs in a machine and the idea that self-interest is the only significant motivator of behavior helps explain why the Army thinks that increasing its "production" of lieutenants, cutting out necessary training for young leaders, and reducing the promotion time to the rank of major will solve its statistical readiness issues with deploying units, meet near-term requirements mandated by the Army and Congress for field grades, and solve potential retention problems.

The ideas of Descartes, Taylor and Root dominated management science and war department circles a century ago, but their ghosts are haunting the Army's human resources command and the deputy chief of staff for personnel. Moreover, the ghosts of Descartes, Taylor and Root will continue to haunt the Army's personnel manager, which filters down to those tasked to develop leaders, as long as Congress shows no interest in rooting out causes of the Army's personnel crisis. This has become a cultural norm defined by the instructor cliché, "teach the basics first."[38]

But Congress and the press are blinded by the sterile promises of another techno-centric analogy – the Revolution in Military Affairs (RMA) – which is based on the idea that war is a mechanistic process and that machines are the true source of military prowess (as if U.S. opponents stand in the open and let us kill them all day). It was the RMA Army that we took to war with Iraq. The RMA is the specter of Descartes, Root and Taylor that haunts the Army today.

There are dangers of reasoning by analogy. Used properly, analogies are powerful reasoning devices because they unleash the genius of imagination and creativity, Einstein's thought experiments being cases in point. But analogies are also very dangerous; on the one hand, they can simplify complex problems and capture our imaginations, but on the other hand, when used improperly, they shackle the mind and take it off the cliff.

Believing that the Army is like a business or that good business practices will solve military problems are examples of misplaced analogies that takes its leaders off the cliff. Effective business practices are often very different from effective military practices. This is particularly true in the area of personnel policies, where the idea of soldierly virtue embodies the ethos of self-sacrifice, and where, as Napoleon said, the moral is to the material as three is to one.

Descartes' and Taylor's management theories were linear, and they impacted adaptability and innovation in leaders by helping to solve personnel shortages, which in turn impacted quality of leadership. Standards in officer accessions (how individuals are prepared to become officers), leader development, promotions and attendance to military and civilian education opportunities, were lowered to meet the need for "bodies" or "spare parts."

There is a mismatch between input and output using this system; namely, officers "punch out" – leave – faster than the equivalent number of lieutenants that get promoted to captain or major based on the predictions by personnel operations research systems analysts (ORSAs) for the future need for majors.

However, why would the combat-savvy junior officers, if not killed or wounded, want to punch out after doing what they had been prepared to do?

The most frequent complaint made by the best and brightest of the numerous lieutenants and captains about departing is that they are frustrated with being micromanaged to death by those immediately above them "trying to make their mark" in a top-down, hierarchal, Power Point-driven culture where junior officer potential for increased responsibility is limited by too many officers "waiting their turn." It is a culture that does not give them enough time in leadership and command positions to do the things they came in the Army to do: for instance, learning the art of soldiering, like troop command and tactical leadership. Even more so, they are fed up with and insulted by the lowering standards that are appearing across the ranks, from which the Army commissions and promotes.[39]

The Army solution: balance input with output by pumping up the input – in this case by beginning to demand more from accession sources. This means that while the ROTC would raise its "mission," but with fewer resources, a higher quality leader is expected. Other solutions imposed by Army include raising the percentage of leaders who are promoted to major (now 99 percent) in an effort to speed up accession rates, and in 2004-2005, sending a few lieutenants into a combat zone without going to Ranger school first, in order to fill "lieutenant slots" in battalions deploying to an insurgency war, as reported by the Army Times. The Army is doing this at the same time it has admitted that warfare today is getting tougher.

A linear approach does two things that are undermining the long-term health of the Army to fix today's problems: in an era of 4th generation warfare, where the Army is asking lieutenants and sergeants to make decisions with strategic implications. First, this becomes a culture that tries to bring control to uncertainty and develops a technocratic culture. Second, a culture that trains and manages for predictability and "one right answer" subdues a leader development system that favors critical thinking among chaos.

The Army's solution is akin to increasing the size of the bilge pump rather than plugging the hole that is sinking the ship. Why is this happening in the 21st century? The Army still views the management of its people through the tired old eyes of Secretary of War Elihu Root and the turn-of-the-century industrial theorist, Frederick Taylor. It has become as acceptable as fish is to water; it's just the way it is done.

The Army's practice to retain officers by promoting them faster aims to solve a structural problem by bribing people to stay – the positive incentive of faster promotions will buy their loyalty, patriotism, and the moral strength to go in harm's way. Yet this kind of appeal to self-interest is precisely the kind of policy that has failed repeatedly in the past and will actually increase the exodus of the Army's "best and brightest" young people – thus robbing the Army's future. It is based on the dehumanizing assumption that its officers (and non-commissioned officers, or NCOs) are mindless, undifferentiated, replaceable cogs in a machine.

The current professional military education (PME) and personnel systems have fossilized into antiquated systems that have long outlived their utility. The Army as an institution is still driven by a "Fordist" mentality of production, quantity over quality, and the Industrial Age military. Also, training has often been confused with education. While the Army created a top notch training doctrine after Vietnam, its focus was on performance rather than long-term learning and retention.

The Army training doctrine – centered on the performance measure of "task condition and standard" – while necessary to support its mobilization doctrine, blurs a distinction between learning (long term) and performance (short term). Its emphasis is on the short term. Much is outmoded and needs to be reworked, rethought, and in many cases, thrown out. Fortunately education theory has advanced, and when combined with a thorough analysis of a history of best practices of leader development, it is now able to provide an answer.[40]

The final problem is that many reforms proposed even today remain solutions that are simply new packages of the same outmoded concepts. The ultimate "fix" lies in reforming the entire system bottom to top (a holistic reform), while a new culture evolves top to bottom. What is needed is a "revolution in educational affairs."[41]

A brilliant Army professor, Lt. Col. Isaiah "Ike" Wilson, Ph.D., now teaching at the U.S. Military Academy, is already leading the way with his proposal to reform the entire professional military education system to deal with the type of conflict that he calls "beyond war." According to Wilson, true Army reform includes:

- Re-tooling all pre-commissioning institutions into adaptive leader programs;
- Establishing a world-class teacher certification course that teaches Army leaders – officers and NCOs – how to teach, facilitate and evaluate adaptability;
- Reorganizing the curriculums of all professional schools to ensure "holistic" (full-spectrum) education;
- Creating a joint and multi-agency Command and General Staff College (C&GSC) system (similar to the British system); and
- Tearing down separate service War Colleges and rebuilding them as "combined" and "multi-agency" educational institutions (civil-military institutions that expose officers earlier to multi-agency team solutions to complexity in war).

This monograph will touch upon these issues articulated by Wilson and his "Beyond War" project.[42] However, first it is necessary to briefly examine the current operating environment (COE) and ongoing Army efforts to prepare for future environments that may be entirely different and even more threatening than today's.

For the last hundred years the people who put these systems in place were trying to do the right thing. Most of them were not evil or corrupt. Time has now passed by today's professional bureaucracy where hierarchic authority, detailed job descriptions, and divisions of work by function are now prominent characteristics. Post-Newtonism recognizes uncertainty and complexity as natural, and now is the time to knock down and do away with the methods that aim for perfect knowledge and performance.

Chapter 1
Adaptive Leaders and Innovators

"Just as training must reflect the hard certainties of the conflict before us, individual soldier and leader education must address its uncertainties. George C. Marshall once said that an Army at peace must go to school. Our challenge is to go to school while at war. The need to teach soldiers and leaders how to think rather than what to think has never been clearer. To defeat adaptive enemies, we must out-think them in order to out-fight them."[43]

Hon. Les Brownlee and Gen. Peter Schoomaker

The Army states that its goal is to produce an officer corps capable of creating an environment of innovation, and a "learning organization" where control is decentralized to the lowest possible levels of rank, in anticipation of highly fluid, complex, non-linear battlefields that have already emerged and will continue to occur in the future. While various Army task forces over the course of the last 30-plus years have intensively studied how to adapt for future conflicts, these efforts will be fruitless if future Army leaders are not properly trained to be adaptive leaders.[44]

Case study: an adaptive leader

The strategic environment in the 21st century will be characterized by a plethora of unconventional and conventional threats involving overall volatility and complexity, and require leaders to be highly adaptive. For the purposes of this study, leaders that are adaptive are defined by the following characteristics:

- Intuitive – this enables rapid decision-making without conscious awareness or effort;

- Critical Thinker – the ability to achieve understanding, evaluate viewpoints, and solve problems;
- Creative Thinker – equally important, called fingerspitzengefuhl, or the feeling in the tip of one's fingers (Napoleon called it a "gut" feeling);
- Self-Aware – an understanding of one's own strengths and weaknesses; and
- Social Skills – the ability to assess people's strengths and weaknesses, the use of communication skills, and the art of listening.

Fortunately, the Army will not have to invent this leadership concept from whole cloth. As the following profile will confirm, junior Army officers serving in Iraq and Afghanistan by circumstance have had to become adaptive leaders through dangerous "on-the-job" learning as they have coped with the insurgencies in those countries. It is the author's contention that the seeds of Army transformation to adaptive leadership have already been sown by necessity in Operations Enduring Freedom and Iraqi Freedom.

Army Capt. Jordan Becker, an infantry officer and 2001 graduate of Georgetown University, provides a good example of what an individual Army officer must learn if he or she is to be ready to deal with the myriad problems of modern warfare.[45]

At the start of the March 2003 invasion of Iraq, Becker was a rifle platoon leader in the 173rd Airborne Brigade, stationed in Vincenza, Italy. Having received his commission as an infantry branch officer through ROTC, Becker had subsequently attended Army airborne training and the Ranger School, where he learned the basic skills the Army teaches its junior leaders.

However, when the 173rd Airborne Brigade landed in northern Iraq on March 26, 2003, six days after the invasion began, Becker soon faced a starkly different battlefield environment than the one for which the Army had prepared and trained him. He was facing the demands of 4GW rather than the industrial-age conflict (2nd generation warfare) that the Army was still structured, equipped and trained to fight.[46]

Fortunately, Becker provides but one of many examples of how junior Army leaders – mostly second and first lieutenants and captains, but also including non-commissioned officers in the ranks of corporal through sergeant – have adapted and succeeded in a 4GW environment:

After he jumped into Iraq a few weeks after the liberation of the northern Iraqi city of Kirkuk, in April 2003, Becker's company commander told him to sort out a problem in Arrapha, a nearby Kurdish neighborhood. Becker, who had brought a bookshelf full of reading material on Kurdish language and Middle Eastern history with him to Iraq, had orders to tell the Kurds in that neighborhood that they had to vacate for security reasons. At the first house that he visited, Luna Dawood, the wife of a Kurdish resident, swore that if the Americans made her leave she would set herself on fire. Becker returned to his base and conferred with his commander, Capt. Jason Ridgeway.[47]

The subsequent encounter was reported by journalist George Packer in an October 2004 article in *The New Yorker*:

They decided that he should try again, but this time Becker, a blue-eyed Southern Californian who is built like a cornerback, left his body armor behind. In this less-threatening guise, he sat down with the family for two hours. "What I learned about these people is that they have a sense of history, and historic patience," he said. "They have a sense of what's best for their community, and when you convinced them that they were going to drive a wedge between their community and the Arabs, and between their community and the Americans, they realized they didn't want to do that." Becker's argument to the Kurds was an abstract one. "If you have a house in a country that's unstable and violent, then all you have is a house. But if you have a house in a country that's stable and ruled by law, then you have a lot more than a house." Then he made his approach in more concrete terms, telling the family, "Just because you won a war doesn't mean you'll get shit for free. If you support law over victor's justice, though, you'll be investing in the future of Iraq." Becker smiled. "And they said, 'That's cool.' "[48]

Another article profiling Becker's experiences in that Kirkuk neighborhood, "Trial by Fire," appeared in *Government Executive Magazine* on April 1, 2005. Journalist George Cahlink described Becker's experience:

After Army Lt. Jordan Becker and his infantry platoon parachuted into Kirkuk and helped seize the Iraqi city in April 2003, they were handed a wholly different type of mission: Solve a local dispute by peacefully evicting families from 67 houses. In the first house, Becker found a cache of grenades, weapons and cash, along with a woman who threatened to set herself on fire if she were forced to leave. The woman, a Kurdish refugee, had moved into one of the houses abandoned by the Arab oil workers and their families who fled or were forced out after fighting began in Northern Iraq in 2003.[49]

Cahlink noted that encounters such as that have prompted the Army to modify its training of junior officers:

Increasingly, the Army is asking junior officers in Iraq to rely more on their own ingenuity than advice from senior leaders or training manuals. The Army is trying to cultivate innovative, audacious leaders for a new era of rapid deployments by smaller units to global flash points. The Iraq war is forging a new junior officer cadre and shaping the overhaul of leadership training.

The key point is this: It was not the ROTC program at Georgetown, nor the Army's ROTC curriculum as a whole, that enabled Becker to succeed at that small but important task. Nor was it the subsequent changes in Army training cited by journalist Cahlink. So what made it possible for Becker to be successful at performing both combat missions and, as the Army calls it "stability operations"?

First, Becker's strength of character gave him confidence. He had the foresight to expand his professional reading outside the Army's prescribed list in military subjects to include studies in Arab culture. As a college student, he had attended the National Security Studies program at the Edmund A. Walsh School of Foreign Service at Georgetown University. There, he took courses on low-intensity conflict, conflict resolution and peacekeeping, transnational relations, and economic aspects of national security. His own self-discipline and formal education prior to receiving his commission set the conditions for him to be able to accomplish such diverse missions.

When Becker was a cadet at Georgetown during 1999-2001, the changes toward teaching adaptability were just being added to the curriculum – to prepare cadets for decision-making and develop their character to deal with the stress and diversity of combat.[50] As Cahlink pointed out in his *Government Executive* article, at an earlier time, the lack of preparation for the changing face of war was systemic to the entire Army, not just the ROTC program.[51]

Becker himself has gained insights on what is required to inculcate adaptive leadership in the Army. When asked what a curriculum in leadership should include, Becker wrote this author that leadership development should provide the opportunity to learn. This sets the appropriate environment for the student to develop adaptability in seeking answers. Lessons may be painful but in a face-saving environment. There should also be a facilitation process that guides the student in how to think critically about the given problem, and finally a place for that student to go to research and find answers. It should close with a follow-on problem or a situation, such as an after-action review, where the student provides answers to his peers and instructor.[52]

Setting the conditions for change

Leaders at all levels of the Army today realize that the service's programs for recruiting and training future officers are out of date. Most importantly, there is growing awareness that true transformation can only occur if the Army culture evolves to establish the conditions that nurture all other changes. Army Chief of Staff Gen. Peter J. Schoomaker has embarked his service on the most dramatic reforms since those of Root in the aftermath of near-disastrous experiences in the Spanish-American War.[53] Schoomaker has advocated parallel reforms across the Army in "17 focused areas" that cover everything from leadership development to doctrine and force structure.[54]

Schoomaker, writing the forward to a recent *Army* magazine article by Brig. Gen. David A. Fastabend and Robert H. Simpson ("Adapt or Die: The Imperative for a Culture of Innovation in the United States Army") described the need to change Army culture as paramount to the other, more traditional changes in strategy and force structure that he has advocated. Schoomaker added: "We must be prepared to question everything. As this article states, 'Development of a culture of innovation will not be advanced by panels, studies or this paper. Cultural change begins with behavior and the leaders who shape it.'"[55]

There are already positive signs of culture change within the Army. Beginning under the leadership of Gen. Kevin Byrnes (and continued under the current leadership of Gen. William Wallace) the U.S. Army Training and Doctrine Command (TRADOC) – which is responsible for preparing officers and soldiers for war – has implemented a number of positive changes that will significantly impact service culture.[56] For example, small changes to individual training for both officers and enlisted personnel now deal with complexity instead of linear situations and solutions. This means that solutions do not come across as a process: visualize a checklist that can be followed with the answer provided if the process is followed – regardless of the environment. Now, soldiers and future leaders are being placed in progressively more complex training situations.

TRADOC has also begun implementing some of Schoomaker's guidance on training, minimizing the long-held emphasis on technical expertise and specialty skill training found among non-combat arms specialties for a more fundamental emphasis on basic soldier skills, such as weapons training, navigation, fire and maneuver, calling for support fire, field-craft, reaction to ambush, convoy procedures and improvised explosive device (IED) awareness, etc. All the more radical is that these tasks, once taught as individual "blocks of instruction," are being introduced as part of training scenarios in the context of lessons learned from Iraq and Afghanistan.[57]

Another TRADOC change with significant potential to shift Army culture is the command's new Basic Officer Leadership Course (BOLC), which features a core curriculum focused on warrior skills and leadership for all new lieutenants regardless of their professional specialty. BOLC training takes place for new lieutenants even before they move to entry-level, branch-specific training formerly known as officer basic course (OBC). General training of all new officers at the beginning of their careers is a marked shift from the Army's tradition of bringing together officers of diverse specialties only after 10 years into their careers, when they undergo training in the Command and General Staff College (C&GSC) program.

In a similar vein, the Army's Combat Training Centers (CTC) such as the National Training Center (NTC) in California and the Joint Readiness Training Center (JRTC) in Louisiana, have already made significant changes to their training scenarios for unit rotations, factoring in the most likely threat scenarios soldiers will encounter in Iraq and Afghanistan built on the "lessons learned" from Operation Iraqi Freedom and Operation Enduring Freedom. In short, the "culture" at the CTCs is evolving from the long-standing emphasis on grading "process and product" to today's call for an emphasis on "results."

The problem with the above changes, however, is that while they are indeed new, and needed by the Army, they occur as a smaller part of a larger culture that is still reflective of a Newtonian, or linear, approach that falls short of the revolutionary concept of adaptive leadership that many say is essential for the Army and its soldiers in the future. The implementation of these ideas into reality will eventually conflict with the larger linearity culture. The adaptation that these acts impart will conflict with the legacy systems discussed later in the text. Legacy systems will diminish the impact these changes will have on the Army.

A key problem is that current efforts to evolve an "Army with joint and expeditionary capabilities"[58] do not address all the problems at hand. Second, the adage, "What we don't know we don't know" can be applied to what was said in response to the question, "Who is adapting?" That is, "For every leader that adapted, one did not."[59] In order to move from a system focused on a 2GW threat to a system that prepares leaders and soldiers for 4GW, the change in approach must be total and almost unrecognizable.[60] Linear teaching methods do not prepare students for a non-linear world.[61]

Army culture as a whole must evolve as other institutions within the service change. Dr. Steven Stewart, one of the original founders of the Army School of Advance Military Science (SAMS) who taught one of the service's few adaptive thinking courses at the U.S. Army War College, cautions: "This is the most complex and hardest thing to do, especially in light of the perceptions of many of illusions of grandeur when applied to the old culture's accomplishments in the absence of critical analysis."[62]

The Army must advance its culture to meet the realities of the 21st century and the post-Sept. 11 world. Merely transforming the Army's organizational structure and design, and keeping in place the methods by which the service trains individually and collectively, will not produce the types of changes that will serve the institution well over the long haul. As veterans – particularly junior officers and NCOs – return from Iraq and Afghanistan, they will re-enter an Army culture that is still built upon a personnel system founded on 19th century management science.

The strategic environment – both the environment in which Army units and soldiers are operating and the domestic environment from which soldiers are recruited – is significantly different today from what it was only a few years ago. Many things that worked previously will not work as well now – at least not without significant modification – including the way the country sustains its all-volunteer force.

Leaving the cultural aspects of the ongoing Army transformation to chance will not produce optimum results; it will be neither effective nor efficient. Through deliberate – not bureaucratic – thought, and by bringing the right people together, it is possible for strategic leaders to guide the Army's cultural transformation in the same way that they are leading the ongoing organizational transformation.

Seven key questions

One of the promises of the science of complexity as it is applied to war is the notion that small interventions can have massive effects when amplified over time. Therein lays the hope for the Army's cultural evolution. There are multiple levers of change, and leader development is a very important one, especially as a culture-enabling mechanism. Even more important are the incentive structures such as rewards and punishments that every member of the organization can see and respond to each day. If culture change can be accelerated, it will occur in part through these highly visible mechanisms.[63]

All of these tools – education, rewards and punishments – affect the most important aspect of "transformation" within the Army: how the Army changes the way it creates and develops its leaders. Looking back on Becker's experience in Kirkuk, it is important to ask what preparation (in education and training), as well as what personal traits he already possessed, which made the young officer an "adaptive leader."

Seven key questions need to be answered in order to solve the problem of how to create leaders who can deal with the future of warfare. These seven questions evolved out of hundreds of questions that I generated researching for *Path to Victory: America's Army and the Revolution in Human Affairs* (Presidio Press, 2002) in 1997, and later refined with the help of Lt. Col. Allen Gill, professor of military science at Georgetown University's Department of Military Science, and Lt. Col. Isaiah Wilson, a professor at the United States Military Academy, West Point. The first five questions address the core issue of how an individual soldier is able to rise above the limits of the current Army culture in dealing with a complex and nonlinear environment:

- What is an adaptive leader?
- What traits must he or she possess?
- Can those traits be quantified?
- What conditions have to exist to create and nurture those traits that an adaptive leader possesses?
- What are the differences between adaptability, agility and innovation?

The last two questions are the most important in terms of changing Army culture:

- How have past and present Army command and control methods restricted and even diminished adaptive leaders?
- Do the beliefs, policies, regulations and laws that shape Army culture support adaptive leaders and innovators?

The following section, and the rest of the report, will explore the answers to these questions.

Defining leadership

"The aim of leadership is not merely to find and record failures in men, but to remove the causes of failure."[64]

– W. Edwards Deming

Leadership can be described as a process by which a person influences others to accomplish an objective, and directs his or her organization in a way that makes it more cohesive and coherent. Leaders carry out this process by applying their personal attributes, such as beliefs, values, ethics, knowledge and skills. Although one's position as a manager, supervisor, or commander provides the authority to accomplish certain tasks and objectives in the organization, this power does not make someone a leader – it simply makes that person the boss. Leadership differs in that it makes the followers want to achieve high goals, rather than simply respond to someone who is ordering people around.[65]

The Army's recent definition of leadership is straightforward: "Leadership is influencing people – by providing purpose, direction, and motivation – while operating to accomplish the mission and improving the organization." (However, at the writing of this manuscript the Army was in the act of changing its definition of leadership.)[66]

Col. Stephen Jones, in his 2004 *Military Review* article, "Raising the Ante on Building Teams," pointed to the contradiction in the Army's definition of leadership:

The Army's definition of leadership specifies two priorities: operating (mission accomplishment) and improving (organizational growth). In practice, however, the Army seldom emphasizes improving organizations. The Army seems to disproportionately reward short-term outcomes while ignoring other important organizational factors relating to institutional culture and command climate.[67]

Given the emphasis on "mission accomplishment" over "organizational growth" this underscores why changing the Army culture is so hard – the Army's very own definition of leadership provides a deep-seated contradiction between the ideal of service and the objective of individual performance that undercuts the very legitimacy of the word leadership.

This is what professional soldiers face today. They attempt to live up to the value of selfless service, but at the same time find themselves driven by bureaucratic personnel regulations (the "up-or-out" system) or policies and practices (a competitive officer evaluation system pitting officers against one another) that force them as individuals to adapt traits that are inherently selfish in order to remain in the profession, i.e. it is better to accomplish the mission than incrementally develop leadership skills for long-term organizational growth.

An understanding of how and why Army culture has evolved to where it is today will help leaders replace the existing flawed structure with what reform advocates term "a learning organization." The current culture, with a reward system focused on short-term results, inevitably creates performers instead of leaders. This stands in conflict with a "learning organization."[68] The Army's current definition of leadership puts a frequently fatal strain on the individual's strength of personal character – which is the bedrock of adaptive leadership. Strength of character is the heart of a good leader.

Character is what you are really like, not the façade you allow others to see. Character is what guides your actions and produces the words you speak. Character is your unique identity, the sum total of your individual characteristics. Character can be good or bad. A person strong in character is someone who stands for what is right, who has the "backbone" to express and live out his or her convictions.[69] Unfortunately, what the Army system too often elicits is not good character, but the bad or selfish version.[70]

Finally, one must understand how education and training are used as complementing components in creating leaders and developing their character. Yet, it is how the American culture uses the word training – as a synonym for education and development – that provides some insight into why the Army today does a good job at training. It is a common Army cultural error to use the word "training" to substitute for education. Both mean something different in regards to cognitive development and the subsequent reinforcement of that development.

Both concepts must support one another in the creation of adaptive leaders. If the Army is to succeed it must embrace the difference between the two terms.

When teaching someone "how to think," it is education; it is training when the aim is reinforcing established ways of doing something. Subsequent chapters in this monograph will provide more details on this topic and how other institutions that know how to create adaptive leaders can provide a model for designing the future Army.

Defining adaptability

In contrast to the linear, analysis-based decision-making process used by today's Army, the service leadership is calling for adaptability. The ongoing war in Iraq and occupation of Afghanistan are forcing leaders to adapt or lose. Adaptability is defined as the process by which individuals and groups decide rapidly, almost instinctively, to changes in their situations. Adaptability and agility are closely related.

Both lead to changes in missions, plans, procedures and outcomes, but adaptability is unimpeded by time constraints. Most individuals, groups and institutions can adapt slowly to changes. Agility, on the other hand, implies a rapid adaptation to changes in a situation. It is this need for carrying out rapid, almost instantaneous change that will determine success in 4GW military operations.

In a recent study on how to train adaptability, "Learning to Adapt to Asymmetric Threats," military analyst John Tillson defines adaptability as it should apply to the Army:

Of the many definitions for adaptability, one seems most appropriate to our study: 'Adaptability refers to the degree to which adjustments are possible in practices, processes, or structures of systems to projected or actual changes of climate. Adaptation can be spontaneous or planned, and be carried out in response to or in anticipation of changes in conditions.'71 ARI [The Army Research Institute] has a similar and simpler definition of adaptability that it developed as part of the course it developed for the Army Special Warfare School. According to the ARI report, 'Adaptability is an effective change in response to an altered situation.'

Adaptability is not the only term used in the context of preparing for asymmetric war. Another common term is agility. One definition of agility is, 'the ability of friendly forces to act faster than the enemy.' Indeed, all of the definitions of agility focus on speed and nimbleness. In our judgment, agility is too narrow a concept to encompass all the factors that seem to be important in dealing with asymmetric threats. While speed or nimbleness is clearly an important trait, we concluded that it was a secondary trait when compared with adaptability. In our view, the essence of adaptability is not speed of reaction, but the slower, more deliberate processes associated with problem solving. As the discussion below will show, speed in problem solving may come because of learning adaptability-related skills but speed is a secondary, not a primary characteristic.[72]

Tillson continues:

Adaptability is a cognitive quality. It cannot be assured by technology alone. Modern technology increases the tempo of war, but it does not assure adaptability. Adaptability has little to do with weapons, munitions, vehicles, platforms, or the things upon which war ministries have labored so long and lovingly. Adaptability has to be the product of people who can face the unexpected with calm resolve while finding ways to turn the tables.

Thus, adaptability refers to the process of adjusting practices, processes, and systems to projected or actual changes of environment, e.g., the situation or the enemy. In military parlance, it also includes the creation of innovative combined-arms organizations, doctrine, systems, and training concepts as demanded by the environment, allies and the enemy. And finally, someone who is adaptive can think of solutions to complex problems in chaotic, unpredictable situations that are based more on intuition than on analysis, deliberate planning and doctrine.

Adaptability in leaders and soldiers is important in the evolving face of war because it is a method of warfare that undermines enemy strengths (this may seem obvious, but most of modern warfare is 2nd generation warfare which involves direct attacks on enemy strengths in order to find the enemy army and destroy it), while exploiting enemy weaknesses by using asymmetric operations (weapons and techniques that differ substantially from opponents' techniques).

The tactics used by adaptive leaders include: understanding rear area operations (4GW warriors do not confront a nation-state's military, but rather its society); the use of, and counter to, psychological operations, such as terror. Further, to solve many of the problems presented by opponents in using these techniques, leaders understand ad-hoc innovation, or the use of the enemy's strengths against itself.

Leaders that are adaptive win 4GW in the moral sphere. Leaders of the U.S. military must understand that the aim of 4GW is to destroy the moral bonds that allow the organic whole to exist cohesively. This is done by conducting menace attacks that undermine or threaten basic human survival instincts. In turn, this creates mistrust that increases divisions between groups (i.e. conservatives and liberals in the United States). And finally, it creates uncertainty, which in turn undermines economic activity by decreasing confidence in the future.

How do adaptive leaders think?

Starting in the 1970s, cognitive psychology began in earnest to question the classical decision-making model and started studying how experienced decision-makers made decisions in "real life" situations. The phrase "naturalistic decision-making" distinguished between this new approach to decision-making theory and the classical approach. While the classical approach studied decision-making under controlled conditions in an attempt remove environmental and intangible factors, the new school sought to study decision-making under "naturalistic" conditions.

The Military Decision Making Process, or MDMP, dominates discussions of decision-making in the context of Army leader development.[73]   The MDMP is a very good example of an analytical decision-making process; it is the first of the two primary decision-making models. Analytical methods such as the MDMP are formal problem solving techniques. The U.S. Army's MDMP is a modification of the French Army's misinterpretation of a German Army decision-making training approach in the late 1800s. In the U.S. Army's model, the decision-maker uses an analytical decision-making process to reach logical decisions based upon a thorough analysis of the mission and situation. The MDMP as well as other analytical decision-making models use the same basic problem solving methodology.[74]

The second type of decision-making model is the naturalistic or heuristic model.

Experience has much to do with this method of decision-making. There are three key steps inherent in heuristic decision-making: experience the situation in a changing context, recognize the pattern of the problem from personal knowledge and experience, and implement a solution. Although this is a commonly used decision-making approach, heuristic and naturalistic models for decision-making have only recently come into prominence in decision-making literature.

Adaptive leaders use the "rapid decision" or "intuitive decision-making" process. The formally recognized intuitive or recognition decision-making approach is simply called the "gut check" in the operating environment. It must be built through a large amount of experience and learning. Adaptive leaders understand and use the "OODA loop" (which stands for "observation-orientation-decision-action") or John Boyd's theory of decision-making, which is a process that relies on experience to recognize key elements of a particular problem to arrive at an appropriate decision. The goal of the OODA loop is to determine and implement an appropriate solution that could result in success more quickly than your enemy.

Adaptive leaders understand "time criticality." In order to make decisions when time is critical, the decision-maker places more emphasis on the intuitive decision-making process than on the analytical decision-making process. Adaptive leaders more readily use intuition, which is to know something without self-conscious apprehension or step-by-step reasoning. In many cases, intuition is directly related to trials and errors through living. There is also judgment in intuitive decision-making, which refers to the ability to match the situation to the first possible solution that is most likely to succeed. However, merely acting on the first solution that comes to mind does not require judgment.

Adaptive leaders also have experience with many problem-solving exercises. An adaptive leader's experience is an aggregate, or combination of what an individual has learned from the process of dealing with problems and making decisions in the course of an individual's career or life. An adaptive leader's education and training builds knowledge that in turn is enhanced by experience. This enables an adaptive leader's ability to carry out "pattern matching." This occurs when an adaptive leader sees similar factors in a current situation compared with a previous one.

The greater the experience that an adaptive leader has, the greater the intuitive decision-making power he or she will also possess. Experience equates to going through numerous problem solving scenarios and learning from them. It does not have to equate to time in terms of a career, but can be based upon how well a leader learns from each intense problem-solving scenario they participate in, can reflect upon, and then verify through research those aspects of their performance they questioned – this is learning.

In the past, it was hoped that the linear system would lead enough senior leaders to develop adaptability over a long career of experiences, and that they would then be able to apply their lessons in times of crisis. In practice, however, the experiences in their career timeline were often not applicable or transferable to the latest evolution of war.

For example what a lieutenant saw and experienced at the beginning of World War I would be different than the experiences he would have during the war in 1918, or what a lieutenant experienced in France in 1944 would be different than what he experienced later if he continued to serve as a senior officer in Vietnam in 1966-67. While some parts of the experience might be transferable, such as close quarters fighting, other parts are not. Whereas reliance on firepower or attrition to defeat the enemy might have worked in one conflict, the same tactics might have negative strategic consequences in the next. Education allows leaders the time to reflect and research one's experiences – to question in order to learn from self-awareness – and evolve as the environment around individuals change.

Today, intuitive skills are reserved for more senior and experienced leaders. The changing face of war demands that these skills must be taught and nurtured in the young leaders much earlier than in the past. Introduction to adaptability and its components begins as early as possible in the leader's career. Developing adaptability, or "how to think," must come to dominate the education, training and selection of present and future leaders.

The new education will develop their ability to pattern match, which is often how adaptive leaders solve tactical problems and challenges in the operating environment. Leaders must be exposed to many learning situations – a loop of experiencing, learning, evaluating, and reviewing.

The OODA loop is not a process[75]
John R. Boyd demonstrated the power of making sound decisions in a timely manner in his theory of decision-making. Boyd contends that human behavior follows a specific decision-making cycle. The four steps of the cycle consist of observation, orientation, decision, and action – what he called an "OODA loop." When two opposing parties are in a conflict, the party that can execute this decision-making process more rapidly and more effectively than the other will gain an advantage over his opponent because the opponent will constantly be reacting to the decisions of the other party. These continued reactions eventually result in poor decisions followed by paralysis of the entire opposition's decision-making process. The common expression of the successful execution of this procedure is called getting inside the enemy's decision cycle.

The critical step in the OODA loop is orientation. In this step, analysis and synthesis of the observations occur. The process consists of taking many disparate nuggets of data and translating them into a mental picture that the decision maker can then use to make a choice. Boyd refers to this as an "examining of the world from a number of perspectives so that we can generate mental images or impressions that correspond to the world."[76]

The OODA loop gains its power from the ability of a leader to form mental constructs. Timeliness and accuracy of decisions and actions relate directly to the decision maker's ability to orient and reorient to rapidly changing and uncertain situations. Personal experiences, education, and training (known also as knowledge) empower the leader to form these mental constructs.

Boyd's theory emphasizes the importance of the ability of leaders to think. By-the-book answers to specific well-known situations are not good enough. It is the ability to think that allows a leader to take the knowledge from personal experiences, education, and training and adapt it to the imperfect information of the present situation to arrive at a timely, sound, and workable solution to that situation.

Applying the OODA loop faster than the opposition is the essence of situational or intuitive decision-making. It is the means of quantifying a mental process into a mechanistic action that all soldiers can understand and apply. Decision-making superiority is merely creating a tactical decision-making base in the operating environment.

While it is necessary to understand the OODA loop, the theory by name should not be introduced as a model or diagram until later in the formal education phase of the adaptive leader's course. As a matter of fact, unless a student makes a direct reference to the process during a discussion, or uses a theory to demonstrate what he or she has just done, theories in decision-making or leadership should not be presented until the latter half of an adaptive leader's course as part of experiential learning, this allows the student to experience it before naming it.

The OODA loop is the better centerpiece of how an adaptive leader makes decisions. Unlike the Army's Military Decision-Making Process – a linear and analytical decision-making approach – the OODA loop provides a guide to how to think faster and more effectively than the enemy. However, it is a guide and not a process. Students should first be guided through many scenarios to discover, on their own, the OODA loop. When finally introduced to the formal theory of the OODA loop, students will say: "Wow, that is what I was doing!"

Consequences of not adapting

Sixteen months after the U.S.-led invasion of Iraq, the U.S. Army War College Strategic Studies Institute in July 2004 published a seminal report on adaptive leadership in Operation Iraqi Freedom entitled: "Developing Adaptive Leaders: The Crucible Experience of Operation Iraqi Freedom," by Leonard Wong.[77]

The critical element of Wong's report was his proposal for what the Army should do with adaptive leaders as they return home from their wartime service:

With a cohort of junior officers experiencing and expecting to be treated as adaptive, innovative, and independent leaders putting pressure on the Army from the bottom, and a chief of staff of the Army familiar with the virtues of special operating forces (not to mention a transformation-oriented secretary of defense) pushing adaptability from the top, the Army finds itself sandwiched between forces of change. The Army can continue the momentum by leveraging and encouraging adaptability and innovation, or it can allow traditional Army inertia to gradually grind down the out-of the-box perspectives of its returning junior officers.[78]

The unacceptable alternative is that these blooded young combat veterans find themselves returning to an Army that develops and enforces traits displayed in poor leaders. It is significant that the current Army culture actually misinterprets Wong's report. As one colonel serving in ROTC replied after this author briefed him on proposals to reform the Army Cadet Command, "But Wong's report says we are doing it right!" The reader must take a critical eye after reading "Developing Adaptive Leaders" and ask why the leaders had to adapt once they arrived in theater.[79]

One Army institution that has remained almost untouchable in the past has been the Army's officer corps, to the degree that it is a taboo even to question its overall quality. It has been equally non-negotiable to question the way that the Army "produces" officers.[80]

One veteran journalist who recently returned from two months in Iraq, was asked, "Did officers adapt?" The journalist replied, "Yes, many were forced to due to circumstances, but at the same time there were just as many others who did not adapt."[81]

Many leaders found that they had to adapt to the unique conditions of a 4GW environment. Indeed, feedback from numerous surveys and interviews done for this monograph showed that an effective system did not exist to prepare Army leaders for 4GW. This failure was not just limited to Army ROTC. As one sergeant major told this author, the Army also does a "poor job" of training lieutenants in units.[82]

The Army must have a holistic reform – from the time they recruit and screen potential leaders through their education and experiences after they become commissioned. Reform must also cover how the Army manages, awards, punishes, evaluates and defines an officer's success. All these parts under what is called officer management fall under the leader development paradigm. Ralph Peters, a well-known military analyst, recently wrote in Armed Forces Journal how the realities of today's warfare conflict with past cultural beliefs:

If there is any single factor our military services neglect that could enhance our strategic and tactical performance, it's the command of foreign languages. How can we 'know our enemies' if we don't know what they're saying?

Although valuable, current foreign-area-officer programs and hasty pre-deployment courses barely scratch the surface of our needs. Officers should be required to develop at least a rudimentary ability in one high-threat foreign language, and superior skill levels should be rewarded handsomely. This goes against our thinking about what an officer should be, but we are going to have to change our thinking as the world changes around us.

A battalion commander forced to rely on a local-hire translator is no longer the most powerful figure in his or her battalion. We will never penetrate our enemy's local codes unless we can enter his mindset, and language skills are the indispensable key.

The reply I got from one four-star general that 'OPMS won't support language training for officers' was fodder for satire. If the Officer Personnel Management System isn't giving us what we need, then we need to change the system. And wartime is the one time when we can do it. To their credit, the Marines are shaping an ambitious language-skills program. The Army must make a similar commitment. Languages are weapons.[83]

What occurs if you don't have a self-motivator like Becker or if the system cannot effectively identify those with the right traits and then prepare them for entering 4GW? Here's how one Army captain responded to this question:

What you get are too many people that should have been screened out early, but for many reasons – an obsession with numbers, lack of calibration between good [ROTC] programs and poor [ROTC] programs, and the fear of political correctness – were not. And with the constant turnover of lieutenants into and out of platoon leader positions, you and your platoon sergeants, and their squad and team leaders waste a lot of time and energy adjusting to and merely filling a big command and morale void [that] poor officers bring to that unit. There are even lieutenants that lack the fundamentals of leadership: decision-making, communication skills and caring for their soldiers. I ask you, how did they get commissioned? I wish someone would tell me.[84]

In mimicking the philosophy of Frederick Taylor and Henry Ford, the Army emphasis on numbers produces varied quality in its officer corps. As commanders must operate under a top-down, zero-defects environment, they compensate for their junior leaders through micromanagement. They are given little time to help their subordinates develop, even if they wanted too.

Meanwhile, the Army can be unforgiving toward fast-tracked battalion and brigade commanders whose subordinates may make a mistake, even in the act of learning. Mistakes are reflected on the commander (and his or her evaluation report), casting a long shadow on the leader's career years into the future. While individual officers may be good people, the system produces a style of leadership where performance under a narrow set of measures is more important than the leadership aspect itself, producing what is informally called a "toxic leader."

Old leader development paradigm

A commander must choose between a negative form of leadership style (using what is called directive style (or micromanagement), or take a risk in developing a junior leader of questionable quality through the use of a prescriptive approach (also called mission orders).[85] As Col. George Reed, director of leadership development at the U.S. Army War College recently pointed out:

"Imagining the deleterious and possibly intangible effects of toxic leaders is not hard. The actual effect on the military in a quantitative sense is not known. In his study of a failed leadership and command climate that resulted in a fatal B-52 crash at Fairchild Air Force Base, Washington, in 1994, Maj. Anthony Kern sagely notes, "When leadership fails and command climate breaks down, tragic things can happen."[86]

The result can be a strategic disaster, as occurred at Abu Ghraib prison when the chain of command did not properly supervise its soldiers. Investigations show that leaders were more concerned with their own careers in complying with what they were told to do, rather than doing what was right under the Army's Code of Conduct and waging war by winning at the moral level. They did not lead or display strength of character.

The officers and NCOs, and the leaders of that unit, according to a report by Maj. Gen. Antonio M. Taguba, failed to lead and demonstrate competence. Unfortunately, similar incompetence wasn't isolated to just the specific unit's command, and may be pointing to a larger problem in the process of how such people throughout the Army became leaders.[87]

Lt. Col. Allen Gill said this in response to the lack of leadership at Abu Ghraib prison near Baghdad: "As a platoon leader, executive officer and company commander, I was always up at night and trooped the line, just so my soldiers knew I cared."[88] Gill indicated that he would have been present to ensure that the acts against Iraqi prisoners would not have taken place, and if someone of his character had been ordered to do that, he would have protested the order up the chain of command.

The lack of leadership at Abu Ghraib had strategic consequences for the entire war in Iraq, and flowed downhill to affect the tactical levels of the war. Lt. Patrick Fagan, leading a brigade reconnaissance platoon in the 1st Infantry Division at the time, said in a personal interview, "We suddenly did not get valuable information through HUMINT because [the Iraqis] were all scared the same [thing as what happened in Abu Ghraib] would happen to them."[89]

A colonel once said in response to these proposed reforms to Army ROTC that "every large organization has an accepted level of mediocrity."[90] By using the S-curve theory, where a level of proficiency or ability is measured against how many resources someone is willing to dedicate for increased effectiveness, one reaches a point that it levels out: no matter how many more resources you place into it, little more is gained. Then, the question arises, how much mediocrity can the Army afford given the "profound uncertainty of the future"?[91]

Conclusion: time to move on

The United States and its allies won the major wars of the past century by developing more highly advanced technologies and deploying them with far superior numbers of troops, on the battlefield and elsewhere, than its enemies. Sophisticated technological capabilities allowed the United States to "reach" into the adversaries' heartlands and destroy their means of sustaining and maintaining their forces. This overshadowed the tactical and operational prowess the Army displayed in the later stages of World War II. Perceived by many, the Army won by "strangling them to death," rather than on the battlefield per se: technology carried the day.

The pervasiveness of the industrial mindset carried over into the Information Age. The United States has developed some of the most technologically sophisticated conventional weapon systems ever known to humankind. The Army won the first Gulf War with them and used them to preemptively enter and topple the government of Iraq. Ironically, the "glow of victory" allowed the Army to justify retaining a leader paradigm that was developed under the umbrella of the mobilization doctrine of the Cold War and before that, of World Wars I and II.[92]

To begin with, one can define the base culture and ethos that the Army must build for the future officer-leader corps as a holistic, professional public service-oriented culture. The service must first build American public servants (professional officers and soldiers), and then add to this cultural foundation a "joint" – multi-service – orientation and ethos. Then, and only then, can it begin to strap on to young officers the military specializations that will define their individual careers (branch culture; battlefield operating system cultures; conventional vs. unconventional cultures, etc.).[93]

The Army must be prepared to evolve its culture parallel to the educational changes proposed in this book. If Army leaders think that they can implement dramatic changes aimed at creating new, "adaptive" leaders while retaining legacy organizations, personnel practices and beliefs based on out-of-date assumptions – while asking the new leaders to "square the circle" simply by innovating – then the entire endeavor will fail.

A new, evolved Army culture must be in place as new officers are commissioned and move into the service. That new culture also must nurture those who have learned how to be adaptive as a result of their service in Iraq and Afghanistan. In both instances, it is imperative that the Army creates an evolved cultural environment to support them.

Large, bureaucratic structures, with rigid lines of authority, are inherently slow to respond and adapt. Adversaries use information technology in innovative ways to decentralize control down to the lowest possible level within cells – shaped by a loose, but commonly defined, mission. The Army has not managed to do so nearly as well. While many leaders and soldiers are adapting, the Army must be honest and ask, "How many have not?" and "How does this impact the mission within the new strategic security environment?" Further, the Army has to see change as a positive reaction, and not a criticism of past and present approaches.[95]

Chapter 2
Today's Culture and Adaptability

"We love the terms 'adaptive leaders' and 'innovation' as long as they do not rock anybody's boat."[96]

- Franklin C. Spinney, March 10, 2005

A new buzzword associated with the Army's ongoing transformation is "adaptive leaders."[97] Another phrase that is a close second on PowerPoint charts or in Army literature is "redefine the culture."[98] This is great news. Publicly stating that the Army is going to achieve these two hard-to-attain objectives admits that the past culture and its supporting leader paradigm is now out of date, and must be replaced. Now action must follow these statements. That is the hard part.

The subject is adaptive leadership. Talking about adaptive leadership is easy, but making it happen is difficult and slow, particularly when it involves the process of screening, selecting, educating and training, evaluating, and finally commissioning individuals the Army believes will be able to succeed in fighting the battles of 4GW.

This chapter starts with analyzing the ways in which the Army has transformed in order to support adaptability in its leaders. It also contrasts these moves with insights into past efforts. Then it dissects the Army's attempts to grapple with defining and trying to set the conditions to evolve the officer corps into a cadre of adaptive leaders.[99] The Army says it is addressing all necessary components – leadership and culture – to move from the Industrial Age into the 21st century (we refer to this as the "what"). This chapter provides a summary of the "what" – the training, education, and personnel management of the leaders that the Army presently has – and the "why," the evolving operating environment that necessitates alterations.[100]

The irony is how quickly things change,[101] and how fast the world is evolving (including the nature of war). A few years ago, anyone who stated that the Army needed to know how to create and nurture adaptive leaders while changing its culture was told that the first objective already existed, and the second one did not need to occur ("things are just fine"). The changing face of war is forcing the Army to at least start talking about addressing the need to change its culture and its leader development paradigm.[102]

It is all too common in the Army – as in many large civilian organizations – that when told cultural change is needed, many respond by praising the advocate for "forward-thinking." For many of these reluctant individuals, the only change necessary to reform the Army is to add more technology, or to tweak existing doctrine or force structure. Fortunately, a growing number of Army leaders, including the current chief of staff, believe that nothing less than evolving the culture can succeed in setting the conditions for success given the changing face of war.[103]

However, how does this belief filter down to those who have to implement those strategic goals and objectives?

The U.S. Army Human Resources Command's Officer Personnel Management 3 Task Force is charged with evolving the way officers are managed in the near term, but its recommendations also influence long-term cultural evolution. The task force's mission is not easy. The members are caught between moving forward with bold concepts (scanned and reviewed by boards of colonels and generals, as well as retired generals or "gray beards"), while also ensuring that soldiers are treated fairly, and most importantly, that the Army remains manned during time of war. Still, there are out-of-date factors or legacies that continue to diminish full Army effectiveness.

Legacies of the Army culture must be changed if the service is to succeed in creating and nurturing adaptive and innovative leaders for tomorrow's expeditionary Army – an Army that is immediately ready to go upon notification, then deploy (move), and be prepared to fight as it lands. The changes should include: (1) the "up-or-out" promotion system; (2) quantity-based accessions, centralized promotion, selection boards and the evaluation systems that support them; and (3) a larger than necessary, top-heavy officer corps – all created under the principle of the mobilization doctrine to mass produce millions of leaders and soldiers in a short time to fight a global world war. Fix these, and the Army takes the first necessary step toward nurturing adaptability in its future leaders.[104]

The history of legacy systems: changing the names but not the substance
"It's the personnel system, stupid."[105]

– Secretary of the Army Thomas White, September 2002

Genuine Army transformation does not stop at changing force structure, battlefield and training doctrine, and buying new equipment. Transformation also requires a fundamental change in how the service manages its people, particularly its commissioned officers. Today's Army Officer Personnel Management System (OPMS) has been in existence since 1971.

Army Chief of Staff Gen. William Westmoreland directed a task force of officers known as OPMS 71 to review how the Army managed its officers. This came in reaction to a pivotal 1970 Study of Professionalism conducted by Cols. Walt Ulmer and Mike Malone from the Army War College. Westmoreland was so dismayed by the results, and indictment on the officer corps in that report, that he ordered it sealed away for 14 years.[106]

As a result of Westmoreland's cover-up, the OPMS 71 task force flatly disregarded the recommendations outlined in the 1970 study. Senior leaders upheld the "up-or-out" promotion system, despite the highly negative review from the Ulmer-Malone report on how that system contributed to the poor performance of the officer corps in the Vietnam War (see below).[107]

The Army War College Study of Professionalism went so far as to state that the Army culture of the time was "one in which there is disharmony between traditional, accepted ideals and the prevailing institutional pressures." It continued:

These pressures seem to stem from a combination of self-oriented, success-motivated actions, and a lack of professional skills on the part of middle and senior grade officers. A scenario that was repeatedly described in seminar sessions and narrative responses includes an ambitious, transitory commander – marginally skilled in the complexities of his duties – engulfed in producing statistical results, fearful of personal failure, too busy to talk with or listen to his subordinates and determined to submit acceptably optimistic reports which reflect faultless completion of a variety of tasks at the expense of the sweat and frustration of his subordinates.[108]

The Study of Professionalism laid bare the military culture that was the legacy of World War II. It found that serving officers of all ranks perceived that if they were to achieve personal success, they had to please their superiors rather than meet the legitimate needs of their troops or develop mission-relevant competence in their units. Many felt compelled to attain trivial, short-term objectives through dishonest practices that seemed detrimental to their unit's long-term goals. The pressure came from field grade and general officers who were "marginally skilled in the complexities of [their] duties, engulfed in producing statistical results, fearful of personal failure ... and determined to submit acceptably optimistic reports."[109]

The OPMS 71 task force ignored all of the 31 recommendations made in the 1970 study.[110] Instead, OPMS 71 increased the power of the centralized, personnel bureaucracy (named the U.S. Army Military Personnel Center, or MILPERCEN, in 1976) with a new centralized Army-level personnel center, which was given even more control. That control, in one case, extended to promotion boards, once the decentralized domain of general officers.

One reason for the resolution to consolidate decision-making was the post Vietnam infusion of women and minorities into the Army, including the officer corps. This concerned the Army's leadership. If the promotion process long delegated to division commanders remained, there was a good chance that the newcomers would be unfairly treated. Army leaders felt the need to ensure that these individuals were fairly treated – promoted and selected on the same grounds as white male officers – and they viewed a centralized promotions board system as the most effective way to guarantee that this happened.[111] In doing so, the Army demonstrated that it did not trust the lower levels of its own culture. Unfortunately, while their intentions were good, that decision created dire long-term effects.

The next modification to the system came in 1985 with the creation of the OPMS 85 task force. The principle outcome was the creation of a "dual-track" system. In addition to their primary service branch (such as infantry or armor), officers would have a secondary specialty – also known as a "functional area"– which ranged from public affairs to foreign affairs or civil affairs. During an officer's career he or she would receive duty assignments in either the primary or secondary specialty areas.

Yet, the traditional image of the officer as a leader of soldiers remained deep-rooted in Army culture, as well as the belief in the primacy of command. With the new two-track system, officers were forced to jump back and forth from their primary military occupational specialty to their secondary specialty. Rather than improving the system, the new plan merely injected an entirely new element of turmoil. This was particularly true if an officer's secondary specialty offered no promotion board command opportunities.

Under the assumption that a secondary specialty with no prospects for command responsibility could not be that important, the system forced the officer to jump back into his or her primary specialty field. Thus, OPMS 85 continued to apply linear solutions when something far more flexible, such as more time in fewer specialties, was required to deal with the increasing complexity of war. The results of the OPMS 85 task force were a step backwards.[112]

In 1996, Army Chief of Staff Gen. Dennis Reimer directed an OPMS XXI review of the service's personnel system. Several external dynamics drove the review, in particular the end-of-the-Cold War military drawdown that would reduce the Army from 18 to 10 divisions. A number of major legislative initiatives passed by Congress also added pressure. These included the Goldwater-Nichols Defense Reform Act of 1986, the Defense Acquisition Workforce Improvement Act of 1990, and Titles VII and XI, legislation for active and reserve components in 1992 and 1993.

Congress' laws created more serious structure-inventory mismatches and demands on an already top-heavy Army. Field grades (majors to colonels) were over-structured. The Army claimed that the 3,400 officers authorized could meet only 75 percent of what the service believed was required. However, these requirements were based on the doctrine of mobilization, when it was expected that many officers were needed to fill new formations for a global conventional war.

Moreover, no one was asking what role the National Guard and Reserve had under this mobilization concept. If the active component was over-filling with field grade officers by placing them in billets to keep them busy until they were needed in the newly raised formations, then what were the Reserves, created for expanding the force in times of crisis, doing?

Of course, we now see that the Reserves were absolutely necessary to meet the force shortfalls in the ongoing insurgency phase of the wars in Iraq and Afghanistan.

Over time, this trend of a larger, officer-bloated headquarters became accepted as a necessary part of a modern Army. Skills were not aligned with requirements – Military Intelligence, Signal Corps and Logistical branches were seen as significantly under-strength. The combat arms officers fill most none-troop (not serving in a unit) positions without a specific specialty, such as ROTC instructors or readiness trainers of National Guard and Reserve units. Other officers were working outside their designated branch or initial war-fighting specialty. The Army refers to these positions with the negative phrase, "non-branch qualifying jobs."

"Non-branch qualifying" positions are necessary to prepare the war-fighting Army for its missions, but are viewed by the culture as a death knell if one serves in them. As a result, readiness suffered as officers found themselves doing a lot more bureaucratic-responsive work appearing to stay busy to satisfy the need to get a perfect officer evaluation report (OER) instead of training for their wartime missions. Also, the great number of officers who needed to become qualified diminished the amount of time any one officer would spend in important positions.

In such a chaotic environment, the Army personnel system pulled officers from primary specialty assignments to meet other requirements too rapidly for the good of the individuals or the service as a whole. One example from the Army of the 1990s was that the service found itself with too many majors. There were a declining number of assignments for available majors that were considered "career-enhancing." This created a queue with a higher demand for majors after their career-essential battalion operations (S-3) and battalion executive officer (XO) time. To meet congressionally legislated requirements, many majors only received 12 months in career enhancing jobs – not enough time to master those positions. The average time for those majors selected for battalion command was only one year in key positions.[113]

The requirement to obtain functional area skills – or secondary skills to their primary military occupational specialties – limited the number of deeply experienced specialists. Worse, almost no officers who focused on these complex specialties were subsequently promoted (except within the booming Army Acquisition Corps). Most officers stayed on the command track, but gained little significant experience while averaging 8-10 years between functional area assignments. Senior leaders recognized the need to develop increased depth in both "war-fighters" and "specialists."

Reimer's OPMS XXI initiative became a four-career field system for field grades where 75 percent of officers served in their operational career function (their primary branch), and the rest remained in their functional area specialty, not switching back and forth as OPMS 85 attempted to dictate. While this system generally worked as intended, the decision beginning in 2003-2004 to impose what was deemed to be restructuring, rebalancing and stabilizing in personnel assignments for unit deployments, threw the Army personnel system into turmoil once more.

Since September 2004, the Army has been conducting a review of officer personnel management systems, including education programs. It includes a top-down analysis of Army requirements for education, while identifying gaps in degrees, disciplines, and the distribution of where officers are located. The review seeks also to identify special skills and disciplines required in the future, and then to recommend a plan for advanced professional education that will enable officers to pass through a "life-long learning" process as their careers continue. At the same time, the Army is looking at changes to distribution policies and procedures – both DOD and Army policies, regulations and directives – while also proposing retention initiatives, and asking how current policies impact soldiers that are not serving in units, but who are pursuing other career necessities to broaden their professionalism (known as the training, hospital and school [TTHS] account).[114]

The Army has identified some key weaknesses in its development of officers, including weaknesses in cultural awareness, critical thinking, pattern analysis, adaptability and self-awareness. Of critical note, observers noted a lack of understanding of irregular warfare, network skills, and how to teach. Also, it was deemed necessary to achieve a balance between the hard skills, math and sciences, versus so-called "soft skills," humanities, where most of the leaders of the Army come from. In sum, the Army is analyzing and proposing deep changes to almost every aspect of its officer management system.

The fundamental problem remains untouched, however. The Army continues to deal with short-term adjustments to an already over-taxed, legacy personnel management system designed to produce officers trained to fight in linear war. Proposed reforms to Army culture still avoid changing the system's legacies, which also serve as the four pillars holding up the cultural structure.

The four legacy pillars of today's culture are:

1. The up-or-out promotion system (instituted with the 1916 Naval Personnel Act, and further institutionalized by the Officer Personnel Act (OPA) in 1947);

2. Quantity-based vs. quality-based officer accessions system (institutionalized by the Morrill Act of 1862 and the National Security Act of 1916);

3. Centralized control of individual performance appraisal and selection systems; and,

4. A top-heavy officer corps and too many headquarters.

As long as these legacies of today's Army culture remain invulnerable, the service will fail to evolve and therefore will not succeed in developing adaptive leaders.[115]

These pillars of current Army culture focus on short-term gratification that surreptitiously contradicts the Army value of selfless service. This forces anyone serious about understanding what it takes to move the Army from a linear system to one that deals with complexity to question whether the service is truly serious about its professed values.

Such a system places all soldiers – but particularly officers – in a climate of conflict between Army rhetoric and reality. They are confronted with the hard choice almost every day: to do what is right, and seek the attainment of hard to-earn, and in many cases, long-term, professionalism, while possibly suffering negative consequences; or, to do what the career system demands, by climbing short-term career ladders without slipping up. In the end, the latter choice will ensure career success, but at a price of being suborned by the system itself.

In a significant study sponsored by the Army War College in 2003, Col. Stephen Jones explained how the culture could fail to align with proposed advances in leader development:

Several adverse trends in command climate have persisted in the Army for nearly 30 years, perhaps because, in practice, the officer culture emphasizes short-term mission accomplishment more than long-term organizational growth, or because Army systems reinforce individual performance rather than organizational effectiveness. Either emphasis, if true, detracts from combat readiness.

Compounding the problem, Army leaders are not taught how to assess or improve command climate nor rewarded when they do so. Army organizations, officers, and soldiers deserve better. Cultural norms and counterproductive evaluation, leader development, and accountability systems are at the root of the U.S. Army's problems regarding organizational (command) climate. Absent a shift in cultural emphasis and adjustment of systems to reinforce the change, command climate will continue to suffer; and unit effectiveness, morale and trust, retention, and commitment will continue to be significantly degraded.[116]

The Army promotion system

The Army pillars include first and foremost the "up-or-out" promotion system. Up-or-out, the requirement to achieve periodic promotion or leave military service is the strongest part of the foundation and in turn supports the other three pillars. Knock down the up-or-out policy and the other pillars will follow. As mentioned earlier in this book, up-or-out was a unique U.S. alternative to European military organizations' professional entrance requirements, a step that satisfied anti-militarism sentiments in American civilian society.

Up-or-out was also an acceptable replacement for the Congress' opposition to the rigorous entrance requirements that the Prussians created to restrict and control access to their officer corps. Creating tough professional entrance requirements based solely on aptitude for military leadership in America was almost impossible in Emory Upton's day in the late 1800s.

The glow of victory after World War II, with the United States having defeated the warlike cultures of Germany and Japan, also made it appear unlikely and unnecessary to reform the system. However, there are aspects of the Germans' education of junior leaders in cognitive and character development that merit examination. Transformation has normally been quicker and more complete for defeated armies unburdened by the legacy of a recent victory. (Nevertheless, the goal of this monograph is not to duplicate a specific doctrine or historical period with that of either a victorious or defeated Army.)

The German approach established the concepts of both professional and individual trust early in the training process, as every officer – through a shared bonding experience – had to negotiate and pass through the same tough standards. This accomplished the creation of a genuine bond of trust within a small but professional officer corps, and it freed the officers to focus on mastering their professions instead of their careers.[117]

The U.S. alternative, while lowering the rigor of initial entrance requirements into the officer corps, created a continual career-long endurance test for those who joined it. This accompanied the Army's move at the beginning of the 20th century to the philosophy of "Taylorism," which focused on "producing" large numbers of officers in the event of a major war.

The U.S. officer accessions process became a rough, never-ending road of short-term performance measures that are far from the standards required for winning on the 4GW battlefield. Up-or-out was created to prevent the appearance of elitism (which other civilian professions such as medicine, engineering and law subtly claim), while proclaiming the façade of equity for all who possess the will to climb.

In fact, up-or-out creates something much worse, as personnel expert and author Lt. Col. Harry Bondy proclaims through his extensive study of personnel management systems:

[The up-or-out policy] does little to improve team performance because individuals do not have a measurable effect on productivity. Legitimacy and commitment suffer because almost everyone not promoted to senior officer and non-commissioned member rank ... is dissatisfied with the current system. Those who are promoted and in control dismiss the dissatisfaction as 'sour grapes'.[118]

Lt. Col. Ike Wilson, Ph.D., who is currently assigned as a professor at West Point, points out an additional result of the up-or-out promotion system in a U.S. Army School of Advanced Military Studies (SAMS) manuscript in 2003:

This author's criticism begins where [Maj. Donald E.] Vandergriff 's ends: the negative and unintended effects OPA 47 and the present officer management system is levying on officer experienced-based learning. The legacy of OPA47 continues to enforce the 'competitive ethic' that derives from a centralized promotion system that, by design and implementation, 'defines success' upon a very small set of critical career-enhancing positions and experiences – command, aide-de-camp (to a general officer), and 'key and essential' staff officer positions, such as Battalion and Brigade operations officers (S-3s) and executive officers (XOs). ... The argument that a 'one size must fit all' approach to officer promotions, assignments, and experiencing is wrought with problems ...[119]

 The second pillar is an officer "production" system that uses never-ending yearly cohorts (the grouping of all officers, of various skills, needed in the Army for that fiscal year) – that in turn creates a "promotion tournament" that undermines trust between officers and encourages negative competition – as if a new automobile model must be turned out yearly in the competitive automotive industry.[120]

The third pillar is the centralized control of promotions and selections based upon individual evaluation systems. In practice, these create the psychological conflicts that counter the values the Army espouses. Bondy continues:

Modern management techniques do not always build good social capital and discipline. Research has shown that individual performance appraisal and selection systems, for example, are inaccurate, unscientific, and prone to sub-group subversion. More than half of any rating variance is due to 'idiosyncratic rater effects' such as how much the rater likes the ratee; whether they have similar personalities; their views on performance; stereotypes on gender, race and ethnicity; self-interest; sub-group factional interests; and variations in work context, which are significant in the military. Most importantly, centralized transfer and promotion queues lead to frequent, expensive postings that reduce social capital, erode trust, and add to careerist credentialism. The annual promotion 'tournament' shifts people between units, as if robbing Peter to pay Paul, primarily to reward the winners. This does little to improve team performance because individuals do not have a measurable effect on productivity.[121]

The final pillar is the top-heavy officer corps. It too has become an accepted truth: the only way of doing business is for the Army and military to possess a high ratio of officers, particularly middle or field grades to junior grades and soldiers. It evolved to the point that both headquarters and laws have been created to justify the officer bloat. However, a top-heavy officer corps is counter to an effective Army trying to operate in a 4GW environment, as veteran defense analyst Franklin C. Spinney points out:

The increasing proportion of officers coupled with the downward trend in force size since the early 1950s means that command opportunities have declined over the long term, and command experience has decreased correspondingly, because command tours have become shorter as we shoveled people through platoon and company-level commands to feed the voracious appetite for officers on the proliferating variety of staffs. This evolution naturally pushed decisions up the chain of command to higher ranks and led to increasing centralization as officers on staffs found it increasingly difficult to justify their existence. Couple that with mobilization-centric personnel policies like the up-or-out promotion system and you have the ingredients for a risk-averse, ticket-punching careerist culture, where self-interest takes precedence over organizational purpose. Not surprisingly, younger people, particularly captains, with their futures still before them, are saying, "This is BS, I'm outta here!"[122]

What the Army must address, and fix, are theses untouchable legacies that lie hidden underneath many cosmetic proposals to educate and train leaders. The problem is that the legacies, particularly the top-heavy officer corps and the up-or-out promotion system, are valued by those within the Army who have the chance to lose the most as they rapidly climb to the top as "unmentionable untouchables." The Army's strategic leaders must have a long-range vision to challenge the legacy systems in order to replace them with pillars that support a culture that encourages and protects adaptive leaders.

Legacies impact adaptability

If anything, recent successes have allowed the Army to continue unknowingly toward a more bureaucratized and centralized organization in light of all the proclaimed and real attempts at implementing adaptability. The four pillars of the cultural foundation are the most potent and subtle social control mechanisms in the Army's previously discussed legacies. These legacies, defined by laws and policies, as well as the culture's criteria of success "have the greatest impact on demonstrating and teaching the values of the organization."[123]

Retention of these legacies provides the primary power levers for changing or maintaining culture. These legacies, particularly promotions and selections tied to the up-or-out promotion policy and individual evaluation systems, presented as inherently fair, determine awards and access to positions of influence and control. They provide specific instructions when tasking subordinates due to an obsession with certainty. The individual as well as the "system" carefully monitor the execution of their instructions, and track all activities and outcomes with the finest attention to detail. Unfortunately, "professional systems and structures are not very adaptable."[124]

If the Army is to become adaptive, and a "learning organization," it must ensure that its personnel system supports its move to adaptability – in people and institutions, and not the other way around, where a retained personnel system limits and diminishes any implementation that results in adaptability. The thread of evolutionary adaptability must exist everywhere. It starts with doctrine and strategic leaders, and filters down to daily activities, threads through policies and beliefs, winding its way from the institutional Army to those forces deployed in the conduct of an array of possible future missions. An environment must be in place to support and nurture the adaptability the Army says it wants in its leaders and soldiers.

Legacies combine to produce an untrusting environment between superiors and subordinates. This in turn necessitates increased supervision, setting the stage for micromanagement. Distrust of subordinates hinders delegation of authority, thereby increasing the amount of information that must be processed at all levels, which in turn slows down the OODA loop (or Boyd decision cycle). Meanwhile, the increased demand for decision-making at the lower levels in a

4GW operating environment force strategic commanders to legislate explicit directions (rules and regulations). As the volume of regulations heaped upon subordinates increase, the overall organization becomes a more rigid mechanical and bureaucratic edifice.

"Method driven orders" (evolving from increased regulation) increase the need for explicit communication between superiors and subordinates. A greater overlap of responsibility occurs, leading to confusion, friction, and competition for authority between superiors and subordinates. Mistrust ensures that tactics are mandated from one level down to the next.[125]

This situation leads to underdeveloped tactical expertise. Commanders treat subordinates less like "thinking beings" and more like slavish, robotic servants. The creative and intellectual ability of individual commanders is underutilized, generating dissatisfaction, cynicism, frustration and low morale. Tactical commanders, given narrow authority, become hesitant to make decisions. The continuous need to obtain permission to execute plans stifles initiative. As they can no longer fluidly adapt to changing circumstances, subordinates become trapped in rigidly defined roles like cogs in a machine and respond ineffectively to a rapidly changing enemy.

Change the pillars and the culture will evolve

"We can agree that what will be needed are more flexible and adaptable officers and a more flexible and adaptable officer corps."[126]

-"Secretary of Defense 2003 Summer Study:

The Military Officer in 2030" Defense Department, Office of Net Assessment Leaders adapt to the conditions of war under the "right" command climates. The conditions of war demand good leaders and commanders to put aside and ignore the pillars of promotion (mentioned above) that drive the internal organizational culture.

What happens when the Army does not adapt to 4GW? As the Army tries to change everything but its culture, a strategic mismatch occurs with an enemy, who continually evolves to its changing operating environment. Boyd said that effective armies throughout history applied a "people first, then ideas, and finally hardware" approach to adapting to environmental changes.

In previous generations of war, the United States relied on a "technology over people" approach that might have led to a tactical defeat or a setback initially, but the nature of warfare and the current global environment allowed the nation time to overcome the mistake. For example, in World War II, once the arsenal of democracy got its production lines going, it overwhelmed the enemy with materials and firepower. Another example is Vietnam where material might and firepower failed to win the war, but the United States was able to recover from the defeat because the lack of globalization and the technology of the day kept the defeat isolated to that part of the world.

Today, setbacks on the 4GW battlefield have broader and deeper strategic implications such as the strengthening of the Iraqi insurgency due to prisoner abuse at the Abu Ghraib prison. Lack of leadership at Abu Ghraib and the policy of treating all Arabs as suspected "terrorists" served to recruit thousands within and outside Iraq to join the insurgency. A culture that understands the evolution of conventional warfare into 4GW approaches warfare differently. The nation may not be able to recover from a tactical set back today.

In order to set the conditions for changing the Army's culture as well as setting the conditions for its new operating environment, it is critical to recognize how change is implemented and where the biggest impact falls. Trust of those at the top of the organization – the strategic leaders – erodes as rhetoric continues, yet nothing really changes.[127] When this happens, trust is replaced by frustration, sarcasm and finally a lack of commitment and acts of self-preservation instead of selfless service. Jonathan Shay observes and chronicles similar cultural occurrences during the Vietnam War in his book, *Achilles in Vietnam* (Scribner, 1994).[128]

Part of the cultural problem involves hierarchical values. It is questionable today whether those at the top of the hierarchy really value something other than those values that led to their own advancement to the higher ranks. Chris Argyris, a leadership and cultural expert at Harvard University, calls the dichotomy of "rhetoric contrasting reality" as "espoused theory," which often differs from the "theory in use."

Pinpointing and understanding the difference between these "theories of action" is a key to beginning a plan to evolve the culture. A lack of this understanding is what frustrates members of the organization who know change is necessary and want to implement it, but over time do not see it occur. They are normally not in a position to impact or influence the change and feel they do not have a voice in the process.[129]

Army culture has been learned both in psychological and social contexts. Hence, culture needs to be unlearned, and then relearned. Many popular management books claim that "re-engineering" culture is difficult because: (1) it is not an engineering problem; and (2) no one knows what the outcome of changing the culture should be. The members of the organization should be suspicious of those inside the culture (especially "those in power") who define the "right" changed culture. After all, they themselves are products of the current culture, raising the question of whether they themselves can be objective in changing it.[130] But the existing operating environments seen springing up all over the world (Afghanistan and Iraq) must be addressed with a new leader paradigm.

The emergence of 4GW demands rapid adaptive decisions from all levels, while understanding the commander's intent, not two, but three levels higher and even farther, up to the strategic level. 4GW also means that knowing how to fight is not enough. Adapting the culture to the demands of 4GW calls for a bottom-up evolution. The ultimate goal is for those at the top to have the strategic vision to "exploit," highlight, and award innovations that will move cultural evolution even farther.

Those at the bottom who must adapt have an idea of what the Army culture should be and are seeing some signs that changes are occurring in reaction to 4GW environments. This happens because junior leaders – officers and NCOs – begin to understand that the key to fighting and winning in a 4GW environment is to understand the three aspects of war – the physical, the mental and the moral – with the moral being the most important. This stands in sharp contrast with an "American way of war" that emphasizes the physical aspect of war (2GW), and the destruction and counting (measuring) of targets.[131]

As mentioned in the beginning of this manuscript some people in the Army understand the dominance of the moral side of war, and this starts at the top with Army Chief of Staff Gen. Peter Schoomaker, as well as other Army officers. Like Lt. Col. Hughes, those who understand the moral side of war use innovations that include non-lethal means to solve tactical problems. This ability to adapt easily supports the type of strategy the United States will have to use to be successful in 4GW. At the very least, these leaders do not negatively impact ongoing missions.

With the exception of the U.S. Special Forces, Hughes' battalion and units like his, and a couple of selected historical examples (such as Gen. John J. Pershing's actions in the Philippines insurrection), the U.S. military has a mixed track record in being able to fight beyond 2GW tactics. A recent 2004 report by Lt. Col. Ike Wilson, III, on the 101st Airmobile Division's operations in northern Iraq, "Thinking Beyond War: Civil-Military Operational Planning in Northern Iraq," supports this inability.[132]

Wilson points out that U.S. war planners and the civilian leadership conceived of the war far too narrowly and misread Phase IV (occupation) requirements. They saw the March-April 2003 invasion of Iraq as the way they wished war would be – quick and cheap in terms of casualties and deployment costs. Wilson goes on to explain how the 101st adapted to stability and support operations in its area of operations. Most successes were due to the adaptations of small-unit and some mid-level leaders such as Hughes. Unfortunately, units that replaced the 101st were not so adept, and the insurgents regained control of most of Mosul.[133]

The Army is just now addressing the mental aspect of war surrounding today's culture from top to bottom. An example of a top-down effort is Schoomaker's insistence that officers and NCOs read books like Lt. Col. John Nagl's *Learning to Eat Soup with a Knife: Counterinsurgency Lessons from Malaysia and Vietnam*. A bottom-up example is the circulation of "lessons learned" by captains who have served in Iraq using the Internet site www.companycommand.com.

To produce adaptive leaders, Army institutions have to become adaptive themselves to evolve current lessons and techniques into curricula as quickly as possible. Today's leader-development curricula are out of date by the time of publication.[134]

The bottom-up approach will take the longest to diffuse through the Army, but it is the best way to change the culture thoroughly and make the changes take hold and stay. For the first time since his death in 1997, articles about Boyd's OODA loop are appearing in Army professional journals such as *Infantry Magazine*. Their authors are not generals, colonels or academics, but rather, young leaders who have recently applied such theories to the realities of 4GW combat in Iraq.

In one recent article, Capt. Aaron Bazin noted, "Many company grade infantry officers have probably never heard of retired Air Force Col. John Boyd, his way of thinking, or his contribution to the art of warfare."[135] Bazin's article shows that he also had the moral courage to publicly deviate from and question the Army's longtime, established and methodical doctrine on decision-making known as the Military Decision-Making Process. Instead, Bazin touts how the OODA loop works well when understood by leaders employing it in the 4GW environment.

Today's battlefield is constantly changing, based more in urban terrain than ever before, and requires a canny ability to deal with civilian populace, to command and control soldiers in a decentralized environment, and fight a tough enemy at the same time.[136] Most significant about Bazin's contribution toward evolving the culture is his use of Boyd's OODA loop in a 4GW environment. He writes:

Faced with new tactical problems set in the environment of Army Transformation, what would an old fighter pilot have to teach us? Simply put, what Boyd can teach you is how the enemy thinks, how you and your soldiers think, how to train more effectively, and how to control your tactical environment.[137]

Bazin continues to show how he and his soldiers applied the OODA loop in combat. The article also deviates from what is commonly found in Army professional journals. Whereas such articles traditionally focused on and proclaimed the correct decision-making processes, Bazin highlights the "observation" and "orient" keys in the OODA loop, with an external focus on the enemy:

The Boyd decision cycle is a way of looking at how people act in their environment. If a commander can train his soldiers to minimize their reaction time to tactical problems, train leaders to make sound and timely decisions, and understand and interrupt the enemy's decisions cycle, he gains the advantage.[138]

Additionally, Bazin concludes that there is a need to actually "train leaders to make sound and timely decisions." But what if these leaders arrived in their units already trained to make rapid and timely decisions because they had received the education to understand Boyd's OODA loop? Bazin is one of many junior officers asking for change, and he is trying to drive the change of the Army culture from the bottom-up through sharing his ideas via professional journals.

Yet, if the Army is trying a people-centric approach to transformation, it will inevitably conflict with the obsession of both the Pentagon and civilian society for high-technology war-fighting and the physical aspect of war. With little focus on the mental aspect of war, U.S. enemies will continue to out-OODA loop (out think and decide) the U.S. military at the strategic level by forcing it to react through its archaic, mechanistic decision cycle to enemy propaganda, threats, claims and actions.

The solution to winning the "global war on terror" (GWOT) lies in adopting a culture at all levels of the Army that understands the power of information at the mental and moral levels. This culture must empower well-educated and trained "strategic lieutenants" and "strategic corporals" who lead and command well-trained, cohesive units.

When Army leaders today proclaim that the culture is changing, they are confusing climate with culture. In Iraq and Afghanistan, leaders are establishing the right climate for their subordinates to succeed. These enablers allow officers like Bazin to come to understand and use the OODA loop. It demonstrates that some commanders "get it," and trust their subordinates enough to let them learn from their mistakes, while highlighting their successes – creating the synergy necessary for victory.[139] It is a mistake for Army leadership, however, to be making claims that such culture change has permeated the service. Indeed, leadership expert John Kotter, Ph.D., states that one reason why strategic leaders fail at changing an organization is because they declare an early victory in the quest to change the organization before real change is in fact accomplished.[140]

At the tactical level, Boyd believed that complexity (technical, organizational, operational, etc.) causes commanders and subordinates alike to be captured by their own internal dynamics or interactions – hence they cannot adapt to rapidly changing external (or internal) circumstances. At the strategic level, maneuver/ counter maneuver tactics would suggest the need for action in a variety of possibilities, e.g. rapid shifts among many simultaneous and sequential possibilities, in order to permit leaders that are adaptive to repeatedly generate mismatches between events and efforts that the adversary observes or imagines. The enemy then falls behind. But, without a variety of possibilities, an adversary is given the opportunity to adapt to events as they unfold.

Another clue may be found in Boyd's "moral war" approach. The Army has to constantly generate mismatches in its own internal culture tolerating personalities that understand how to win in a certain environment, while appearing odd or eccentric in other environments, such as the home front. Rather than micromanagement from above, the answer is a bottom-up approach focused on achieving the commander's intent. The challenge is to overcome the culture's dependency on actions of senior leaders (signals) that the members of the Army then follow. As the Army continues efforts at transformation, it will be critical to determine whether changes are "people-centric" or whether they remain "technology-centric."

Conclusion: the U.S. Army of 2020
"The best way to anticipate the future is to create it. The Army is moving out, and this is merely the beginning. Our incentive is not change for change's sake. Our incentive is effectiveness in this protracted conflict. If necessary to defeat our adaptive adversaries, the changes described here are a mere down payment on changes that will follow." [141]

–Hon. Les Brownlee and Gen. Peter Schoomaker

Newtonian linear warfare still defines today's personnel management laws and policies. While these policies were necessary at one time, they are becoming less and less relevant in the post-Industrial Age. Today with the quality of the members of the Army so high, why is it necessary to cling to policies, laws and beliefs whose origin lay with assumptions about people made over a century ago for organizations comprised of less-educated and poorly trained members?

These legacy systems have long outlasted their value.

A precondition to reforming the way in which the Army develops, creates and nurtures adaptive leaders will be to completely reform the service's personnel system. While the Army has started to create and preserve unit cohesion by stabilizing assignments and showing leaders "what 'right' looks like," the system will also have to eliminate up-or-out promotion (and the careerism it mandates), while significantly, but slowly, reducing the size of the officer corps above company grade ranks. The latter reform is of central importance for "flattening" Army organizations by both reducing the number of headquarters and making those that remain much smaller. Calls for decentralization that do not reduce the number and size of headquarters are empty rhetoric.

In turn, moving from up-or-out to a new promotion system will demand that accessions – how a U.S. citizen is made into an officer – become tougher. Earning the right to become an officer should be based on a rigorous selection – display of mental and physical stamina – without regard to "making mission." Institutions charged with this important task should be judged based on the quality of their alumni, not by how many officers they "produce" to meet statistical objectives. Adaptability will be present in the accessions selection by testing all who aspire to become leaders for their ability to deal with uncertainty, while under stress. The cultural theme should become: "Better no officer than a bad officer." Or more broadly, "Better no leader than a bad leader," as it applies to non-commissioned officers and civilians.[142]

Finally, evolving the Army toward a learning organization will necessitate blurring the lines between bureaucratic authority and bureaucratic responsibility, both of which pervade in the institutional Army. Real change threatens those comfortable with their current ways, the unambiguous structure of work, power and responsibility. If the institutes are reformed, many would see their authority and status threatened and their careers would become less secure. There may even be anxiety and confusion about social rules of interaction as lines of authority become more ambiguous.

Despite rhetoric to the contrary, many supervisors do not want more autonomy for their subordinates. Moreover, many workers and soldiers do not crave more autonomy in their jobs if it comes at the price of unclear performance expectations and the loss of insulation that strict rules provide. Employees and soldiers in large Army and government headquarters are comfortable with the predictability and safety that the structure of their work provides. Many people prefer to be led. This situation must also be addressed prior to becoming a learning organization.

The point is that the Army has to do more than just put the word "adaptive" and "leader" on Power Point slides or highlight it in official literature. There are many concrete steps that can be taken to create adaptive leaders, beginning with modifying the education and training of the Army's cadets, junior NCOs, and entry level civilian managers. Cultural change is a long-term evolutionary process; the spark starts at the beginning of leaders' careers.

The Army that the nation needs to fight in and win in both 3GW (maneuver warfare such as demonstrated in the March-April Army and Marine drive to Baghdad) and 4GW environments will begin with a leadership development revolution. Nothing is sacred if it is proven irrelevant in current or future operating environments.

It will take a true national team effort involving Congress and the American public to both persuade and empower the Army to create a true "learning organization." The culture of such an organization needs to be based on the idea that what worked yesterday might not work today, and almost certainly will not work tomorrow. Failure to change may even lead to defeat if past approaches are adhered to simply because "It was the way we did business." To succeed, Army leaders must stop regarding criticism (if it is based on sound principles and research) as disloyal, and must actively encourage critical thinking. Establishing and practicing trust involves more than rhetoric.[143]

Unfortunately, the next war is today's war and its conditions are different from those for which the Army is currently structured, organized and prepared to fight. On top of that, the current personnel system is built, designed and culturally prepared to "manage" personnel in an Industrial Age manner. As the international security environment continues to change at an increasing pace, the Army must match that via genuine transformation efforts based on revolutionary ideas.

The ultimate factor in determining how successful transformation will be is how well the process is championed from both the top-down and the bottom-up perspectives. Change in any large organization takes time, and when an organization's culture resists the required change, the time it will take will be even longer.

It is in the best interests of the Army, and the nation as a whole, that all Army officers agree to curb parochialism and cultivate an Army culture that maximizes the benefits of transformation. This will be the true test of selfless service, and without it the Army and its soldiers cannot evolve to fight and win in 4GW.

Chapter 3
Creating Adaptability

"Future battlefields require a more liberally educated, mentally adaptable leadership to coexist in a culture with high standards of cohesion and discipline. An adaptive Army will require very high standards of entry training for commissioned members, to acculturate tactical knowledge in the force at a very early stage."[144]

Col. Robert B. Killebrew, U.S. Army, (Ret.)

Members of the Army, including senior officers, must continually evaluate how to make Schoomaker's response of "at what?" too many assertions that "The Army is the best in the world," a true statement.

While the U.S. Army has proven itself time and again adept at training soldiers and officers for 2GW, we have shown that training is far less vexing a challenge than educating. To be the best in the world, today's Army, and the Army of the future, needs leaders that are adaptive – meaning leaders that persistently question their organizations practices, and adhere to the belief that there is always room to improve.[145]

There are positive signs that learning from recent experiences is occurring, but the Army continues to be hampered by a system that is based on Industrial Age concepts of warfare. The Army's recent rhetoric indicates that its leaders recognize the need for cultural change, such as a need to further professionalize its officer corps, but there remains a noticeable gap between rhetoric and reality. Implementation of specific changes in education and culture must happen more quickly.

Current leadership development programs are still based on the dated assumption that there is significant time to train leaders after they receive their commissions, but this is not the case in a 4GW environment. This outmoded premise must be jettisoned. The leadership educational program must become more academically rigorous to ensure that commissioned officers are as qualified and prepared as possible.

Also, 4GW operating environments require that the Army develop leaders prepared to deal with an array of new threats. The future Army faces the task of operating against new methods of warfare practiced by multiple state and non-state opponents. Future opponents will also be equipped with both government-procured and off-the-shelf technologies as sophisticated as those of the U.S. Army itself. That is, 4GW has the ability to level the playing field for many opponents without great expenditures on resources.

Soon, moreover, the U.S. Army may also find itself without a limitless pool of resources. Demographic and socioeconomic factors will be a leading cause of strain on the Army's personnel resources – such as the aging baby boomer generation entering retirement that is beginning to demand a larger share of the nation's wealth – and national and international businesses will continue to compete with the Army for talented people. The latter competition will be critical, for the Army will require truly top notch individuals both to teach a diminishing pool of potential leaders and to populate that pool.

John Schmitt, a co-author of a critical *Marine Corps Gazette* article in 1989, described the new complexity of war this way: "War is fundamentally a far from-equilibrium, open, distributed, nonlinear dynamical system highly sensitive to initial conditions and characterized by entropy production/dissipation and complex, continuous feedback."[146] With that observation in mind, how the Army creates adaptability must also evolve as the service deals with the complexity of 4GW. Schmitt's work with complexity theory as it applies to war can also be applied to the education and training of leaders.

Rather than teaching decision-making and leadership in war as a stable structure, as Schmitt argues, the Army needs curriculums to deal with a type of war that "resembles a standing wave pattern of continuously fluxing matter, energy and information. War is more a dynamical process than a thing."[147] According to him, the Army needs to change the way it addresses the professional education of leaders.

As an example, teachers at any leader-centric course should "refer to Army operations or mission as "evolutions," a term that has biological connotations rather than mechanistic ones. This suggests that the theme of curriculums, which deal with leader development, should be "adaptation and adjustment" rather than "precise planning and detailed schedule" curriculums and training plans that "enforce" procedures.[148] In contradiction to established beliefs, a new model of leader education would depart from current conditions where 1) students often know everything about the course before hand, and 2) there are expectations about orders, lectures, pressure for constant feedback and a preference for performance over learning.[149]

The bottom line is that an adaptive course model (ACM) must begin with trust acquired between professionals who have already passed through significant, tough entry standards as an officer and NCO, and are further screened, selected and certified to teach and develop adaptability.

How to forge adaptability in Army leaders and culture
An effective solution is for the Army to establish and implement an adaptive course model (ACM) at one or more of its institutions that deal with its leader development as well as its operational units. The obvious institutional choices are those that deal with the development of cadets and lieutenants. As the ACM gains acceptance, the Army should look for other opportunities to introduce this educational and leader development model.

Discussed in this chapter are the major elements of how to develop adaptive leaders for the future. They include: (1) the adaptive course model (ACM); (2) the ACM Program of Instruction (POI); (3) the establishment of teachers of adaptability (TA), through a certification process and implementation of tools they can employ to develop adaptability; and (4) the Leader Evaluation System, or LES. Taken together, they form the beginning of the new leader education revolution.

Adaptability Course Model: a first step to change

The ACM should be applied horizontally at any level of the officer education system (OES), as well as to NCO and Army civilian education systems. Such a model provides guidelines that include: how students are taught and evaluated (metrics), how senior-level leaders are created and taught to think about strategy and running large organizations and, its most important feature, how individuals are selected and certified to teach. The ACM is the Army's answer to instituting a process that moves beyond its vision to a tangible method to instruct its leaders "how to think" rather than "what to think."

Army leader-centric institutions or operational units should introduce the ACM as they evolve their organizational environments into learning organizations. This is important because it does no good to have a great teacher of adaptability if the command environment and the overarching Army culture remains stuck in the Industrial Age, playing the role of enforcer rather than supporter.

Institutions or units can apply ACM with no additional resources and without lengthening the time given to today's leader-centric courses. The ACM takes advantage of the insights and experiences of the Army's pool of combat veterans. It also requires their continued initiative and desire to train and help grow future leaders.

The ACM is a cultural change, and not a prescribed list of tests and exercises, or stringent lesson plans and schedules. The ACM builds on the Army's core principles and values referred to as "warrior ethos" developed in 2003. Warrior ethos is defined as:

- The foundation for the American soldier's total commitment to victory in peace and in war;
- Exemplifying Army values, putting the mission first, refusing to accept defeat, never quitting, and never leaving a fallen comrade behind; and
- Absolute faith in oneself and one's team.[150]

The purpose of the ACM is creating leaders who understand and practice adaptability, while encouraging Army senior leaders to nurture this trait in their subordinates. A student that emerges from any leader-centric course that employs the ACM is adaptive and can demonstrate the ability to:

- Rapidly distinguish between information that is useful in making decisions and that which is not pertinent;
- Avoid the natural temptation to delay their decisions until more information makes the situation clearer, at the risk of losing the initiative;
- Avoid the pitfall of thinking that once the mission is underway, more information will clarify the tactical picture; and
- Feel the battlefield tempo, discern patterns among the chaos, and make critically important decisions in seconds.

The ACM also develops the following traits:

- Strength of character;
- Experience and intuition through repetitive skills training;
- An understanding of the value of self-study; and
- Proper understanding of a command climate that promotes adaptability accepts change and encourages innovation.

The ACM is comprised of three elements that will enable a leader-centric development institution to achieve the goal of producing leaders that are adaptive. These consist of: (1) an Army culture of learning, which includes a chain of command and offices that oversee leader-centric institutions and operational units; (2) a curriculum significantly broad to provide the necessary cognitive and creative development to nurture adaptability; and (3) highly qualified teachers. All three must exist in concert in order to effectively enable adaptability in students attending the course.

First, establishing an ACM primarily requires creating a "learning organization" with a climate that frees its instructors to focus on what is important: teaching, facilitating, mentoring and evaluating a student's grasp of adaptability. As Brig. Gen. David A. Fastabend and Robert Simpson relate, "the learning organization overcomes the impediment of centralized responsibility by instilling within the organization's members a thirst for creativity and hunger for a challenge."[151] It will require a thorough understanding of education and training, as well as what defines learning, or the acquiring of knowledge.

The ACM, occurring within a "learning organization," will allow students to:

- Experience the emotional trauma of failing within a safe, face-saving environment; and
- Find answers for themselves and build intuition – a necessary trait of adaptive leaders.

The learning environment also supports and understands that the ACM is where students become members of the course when they are:

- Left to do as much as possible, from planning training to making and executing recommendations to improve the course;
- Allowed to fail, as long as they show signs of learning, and do not repeat mistakes (those who made a mistake in the act of doing something will attempt to explain why they made their error); and

- Pushed to seek answers, and to produce adaptive leaders familiar with tasks that may comprise their solutions to tactical and non-tactical problems. They understand how to employ tasks together to solve problems.

The Army as a learning organization supports the ACM by creating avenues for the teacher of adaptability to access, share and assimilate information. In fact, the Army has alluded to the need to streamline its information flow:

To that end, the Army will continue to refocus institutional learning, shifting Center for Army Lessons Learned collection assets from the CTCs to deployed units. Similarly, recognizing that a learning organization cannot afford a culture of information ownership, the Army must streamline the flow of combat information to assure broader and faster dissemination of actionable intelligence.[152]

The Army can use its distributed learning information systems to free the ACM from many mandatory requirements usually conducted during the initial phases of courses, or that take people away from training in an operational unit. This is where the first test of adaptability – ethical conduct – can occur, especially for students of leader-centric courses. Students can use the Internet to conduct most processes – download, read, then sign and return – as well as knock out many mandatory briefings that are required by law, regulation or policy, which traditionally could only be done in a lecture format. This course of action returns responsibility back on the shoulders of the student, while providing a more efficient use of time and resources for conducting scenario-based education, which will be discussed in forthcoming pages.

Using the Internet to execute many administrative tasks and mandatory events also frees up the TA's time. In a "learning organization," the TA's focus must be on cognitive development in order to better teach critical and reflective thinking among students. This will replace the now almost total emphasis on the "what to think" content that permeates competency-based education environments. Developing leaders with a deeper understanding of decision-making will conflict with those who continue to advocate the approach of mastering and revisiting the basics in creating tacticians and managers.

A major change in the leader development paradigm takes place by introducing cognitive development through the experiential learning process in the beginning of an aspiring leader's professional development. The challenge is achieving a balance between cognitive development and task proficiency, but it can be done when they are viewed in concert and not as separate approaches to leader development. The use of decision-making exercises and the placing of responsibility on the shoulders of the student occur as early as a cadet's freshmen year in college, or as a junior non-commissioned officer attending their first NCO course, or as a civilian beginning their first management course.

Accomplishing this change will stand in contrast to established beliefs regarding "teaching the basics" through rote memorization of the technical aspect of the profession also known as "task-training." The new leader development paradigm starts with developing the leader – the hard part – first, and then the technician later, once the leader knows how to think.

ACM Program of Instruction (POI)

The POI deals with war as it really is – a complex and open environment – wherein teaching is a process of continuous adaptation. The goal is to put the student through a course of continuous adaptation to changing situations of growing complexity. Development of leaders today must parallel real-world operations that do not proceed with clockwork mechanics as "operations," but are instead "evolutions" along the "edge of chaos."

The POI evolved from an educational approach developed by a Swiss educator named Johann Heinrich Pestalozzi.[153] He developed his theories on education in the late 1700s, based on the concept that students would learn faster on their own if they were allowed to "experience the thing before they tried to give it a name." More specifically, the POI uses Pestalozzi's methods to let students have an experience that identifies a problem, and then lets the student deal with that problem without "wasting time working their way to finding a solution," according to Dr. Bruce I. Gudmundsson, author of several prominent military history books dealing with military effectiveness and an consultant to the United States Marine Corps.[154]

The POI does not operate from the top of the institution toward the bottom. The POI, curriculum and lesson development deals with complexity as an adaptive process. Top-down guidance should only be used to encourage a few core principles like adaptability, intuition, self-awareness, critical thinking, creative thinking, and strength of character.

The POI uses experiential learning to build student experience using the "recognition primed" decision-making process. The POI consists of four primary curriculum pillars, revolving around scenarios (known today as training packets) that use the experiential learning model that enables adaptability in a continual learning feedback loop, including the use of: (1) a case study learning method; (2) tactical decision games; (3) free play force-on-force exercises; and (4) feedback through the leader evaluation system (LES).

A wide variety of educational methods chosen by teachers support the curriculum pillars of the POI, and they allow students to gain a greater benefit from their educational experience than without the POI. The academic methods employed in support of the pillars include: small group lectures, small group training exercises, exercise simulations, staff rides, and private study (encouraging access to information). These aspects of the curriculum mutually reinforce one another by providing a holistic outlook toward problem solving while building the student's character.

A final, yet important aspect of the POI is the use of the continual learning feedback loop through use of the leader evaluation system, which emphasizes After Action Reviews (AAR, or peer and subordinate evaluations) and continual observations by certified TAs, with the emphasis on allowing students to discover the answers to various scenarios for themselves. Through each pillar and method, the TA facilitates the student's quest for learning through the art of asking questions, much like the Socratic teaching method.

The TA can use this method in conjunction with any tool that is used to deliver a scenario. Webster's dictionary defines the Socratic method as the "systematic doubt and questioning of another to elicit a clear expression of something supposed to be implicitly known by all rational beings." The TA uses the Socratic method to pick at a student's thought process in order to get the student to explain their rationale in solving a particular problem. The TA can do this during the team AAR, but it is preferable to use this method during the conduct of a tactical decision game (TDG) or during individual counseling.[155]

From the beginning to the end of the ACM, students are always in a leadership role, with an assigned mission, guided by a commander's intent two levels up. Throughout an ACM, a student should be observed having to make decisions in several scenarios in order to see if they understand and demonstrate adaptability.

Another aspect of the POI is that it introduces theory after experiential learning. The Pestozzoli learning method, which exposes students to problems "above one's pay grade," and similar teaching methods, pushes students to discover and experiment. Students' first test their own problem solving methods in different scenarios, and then at some point afterwards teachers should introduce specific theories to them. Most of the time, students will respond, "Wow, that is what it is called!"

The POI unifies the approaches above in accomplishing ACM learning objectives, which include:

- Improving one's ability to make decisions quickly and effectively;
- Making sense of new situations, seeing patterns, and spotting opportunities and options that were not visible before;
- Becoming more comfortable in a variety of situations;
- Developing more advanced and ambitious tactics; and
- Becoming more familiar with weapons capabilities, employment techniques, and other technical details.

The POI uses training as the reinforcement of the education that has occurred during the four aspects of the curriculum. As cognitive abilities are established, task training is brought in to reinforce and provide multiple tools to assist leaders in their decision-making. Education is intellectually intense, while training is resource intensive. Put another way, training for most military tasks calls for resources such as ranges or training areas, and equipment such as weapons or vehicles. Planners can amass limited resources in a centralized location, such as an Army post, to efficiently support task training to allow for effective execution.

Education, on the other hand, can require little more than a classroom. At the core of cognitive education is perhaps the most limited resource – a good teacher who can teach and facilitate learning. A teacher must possess the skills to mentor each student to do better, while also evaluating his or her ability to adapt. A teacher must also have the moral courage, combined with knowledge and experience, to tell a student – and the appropriate chain of command – that he or she will likely not succeed in combat leadership.

The remaining key factor in creating adaptive leaders through the POI is learning. Potential adaptive leaders must be able to assimilate the education with their training and apply both through their personal actions. Learning is a measurement of whether the adaptive leader is ready to practice in the real environment what has been preached in the classroom.

At the individual level, finally, there is no substitute for experiential learning, and today's Army is the most operationally experienced Army in U.S. history. There are tremendous opportunities to leverage experience through the Army's well-developed training doctrine of AARs, lessons learned, the great experience of the serving officers and NCOs, and the links from joint and Army operational analyses to formal learning – distributed and in the classroom.

At the same time, some of the best battlefield lessons result from tragic but honest mistakes. The Army cannot allow a zero-defects mentality to write-off those who make such mistakes. And we should review our leader evaluation systems to ensure they are leader development tools and not merely management sorting tools.[156]

The POI begins the development of adaptability through exposure to scenario-based problems as early as possible. The POI should put students in tactical and non-tactical situations that are "above their pay-grade" in order to challenge them. Evolution toward adaptability starts at the very beginning of an individual's quest to enter the profession of arms. The POI examines scenarios based on historical examples through case study learning. Tactical decision games, or TDGs, for instance, consisting of both tactical and non tactical situations, and free play force-on-force exercises, are tools that sharpen decision-making skills and provide a basis for evaluating students on strength of character.

A reoccurring principle involves mentorship through either AARs or one-on-one mentorship. As discussed below, students should be evaluated based on how they went about solving a given problem, not the solution itself.[157]

An ACM training calendar and supporting weekly schedule should not consist merely of blocks of training crammed into every hour of the day. The ability of students to attain adaptability traits should determine when learning ends. Since being adaptive is dealing with the unknown, a calendar and weekly schedule will provide little illustration to the student on how to prepare for the unpredictable. Teachers could instead use a calendar deceptively to help encourage adaptability by changing events listed. Schedules are mainly used by TAs to determine the length of time – preparation, conduct and feedback – a scenario may take using different delivery tools.

The ACM calendar resembles a vertical stream with branches running horizontally across the pages of the calendar. Teachers use them to guide their preparation periods, which include a great deal of detail, and it helps estimate the amount of time teachers may spend with students. Achieving the learning objectives of the scenario drives such activities, and those who have successfully taught adaptability say that every hour conducting scenarios with students demands three hours of preparation and "close out time." Close out time includes updating student records with the latest observation cards, any unplanned individual counseling, and reviewing the conduct of the scenario in order to improve the experience in the future.[158]

Weekly schedules also list key events where teachers must come together to pool their resources, rehearse and conduct leader reconnaissance to make the educational experience for the students as rich as possible, such as the conduct of free play force-on-force training. Weekly schedules may also provide "aiming points" showing when students should attain a certain level of understanding of adaptability. These should be accompanied by formal counseling sessions.

One of the major concerns by people that have been briefed on the ACM is achieving a balance between the experiential approach of the ACM and other, more tangible "requirements" that currently dominate today's leader centric courses. The tangible requisites include proficiency with one's weapon, the Army Physical Fitness Test, and other "graduation requirements" set by a commanding officer, regulation or law such as equal opportunity and sexual harassment briefs. As mentioned earlier, these duties can be fulfilled by employing the Internet. Many individuals believe that you can only accomplish one or the other, but this is not true. The ACM merges these requirements with the principles of the ACM without diminishing the standards or requirements to meet them.

Teaching adaptability requires that resources previously used to enable adaptability remain as simple as possible, and continue to support the use of scenarios. The systems supporting it, from the LES tools, such as the observation cards used by cadre to capture their observations of student performance during scenarios, to the planning for training so logistics won't take time away from the conduct of scenarios, should also remain simplified. Teachers must be free to focus on the development of adaptability over time or "evolutionary adaptability" based on numerous observations of students involved in several different scenarios under various conditions.

As an illustration, if an ACM teacher plans to use real M16A2 rifles with blanks and a multiple integrated laser engagement system (know as MILES, or a laser simulation of real bullets), without taking into account the time it takes to sign for, pick up, travel, issue and zero, then little or no adaptability will be enabled. There is value in using this equipment, especially in a free play force-on-force scenario, but an instructor should balance their use with the development of adaptability. Principles outlined in the ACM also mix with traditional "requirements" or graduation standards.

The planning, preparation and execution of the M16A2 rifle range is a good example of a training event that is task-centric. We all agree it is essential for "warrior leaders" to be proficient with their small arms. The students like to shoot. Teaching and evaluating marksmanship and range conduct, however, limits adaptability. Or, does it? This task does not have to be cadre-centric. There is room to enable adaptability, but it will take planning and an open mind to find that balance.

Some have wondered whether in the process of encouraging adaptability, cadre overseeing the POI would allow accountability and responsibility to suffer. A colonel recently lamented it would be "students running wild under no one's control."[159] This is perhaps one of the greatest challenges faced by a TA, balancing the need for adaptability while holding the students accountable for their decisions and actions. First of all, ethical conduct must be maintained. The POI emphasizes that inflicting stress through a variety of methods will expose weaker students' unethical conduct. It will be one of the first breaking points among students. If students respond to questions with inaccurate situation reports, TAs should not tolerate those who lie, cheat or steal.

Students should be held to high standards in maintaining their physical well-being and equipment. This aspect holds true with unit and leader-centric institutions that deal with junior leader development. Discipline serves as the baseline to create conditions to practice adaptability. Students must realize that it takes discipline to retain them as the course progresses into and through stressful field problems.

For example, students were tasked during a ROTC brigade field training exercise to maintain sanitary conditions of their dining facility while they were in garrison (staying in barracks). The cadre explained the reasons for the task and how it would relate in war. When their students failed to organize and plan to maintain the cleanliness of their facility, the use of the facility was taken away from them. The students were forced to eat meals ready to eat (MREs, which evolved from c-rations) outdoors until they came up with a plan to meet the requirement. The students realized that if they could not keep the dining facility clean under peacetime conditions, then what would happen in the field? They learned that their lack of discipline and teamwork would bring in rodents and insects causing disease and degrading their ability to accomplish their missions.[160]

During another mission, student leaders were tasked to move to a military operation in urban terrain (MOUT) site to conduct free play force-on-force platoon level exercises. Student leaders had been given their operations order 12 hours prior to a move time of 7:00 a.m. the next morning. While there was a lot of work to be done to get 220 students reading, moving, properly led and planned, and supervised while tasks were accomplished, it was possible in a 12hour period. In the excitement of wanting to do the force-on-force training, the student leaders dismissed or forgot crucial personal and equipment checks (to ensure they had everything they needed or might need).

Prior to the student company loading on trucks to move out, TAs stepped in to ask the student leaders whether these checks – referred to as pre-combat checks – had been conducted. All but one of the students in key company and platoon positions indicated they had not; it had been left to the individuals to make sure they each had what was spelled out in the unit SOP. (The one student, who filed a false report, in the role of platoon leader, was relieved and counseled regarding his unethical conduct.) At this point, the TAs of the student leaders questioned them on what actions they should take so they could be ready to go to the training, if they were not already prepared. When the students responded with the right answers, the TAs adjusted the schedule to allow the students to do the right thing.[161]

The POI encourages the Army to consider preparing leaders for war in more innovative terms, which in turn points to a different overall approach to Army education. It is an approach that does not pursue certainty or exercise precise control. However, it will create leaders who are able to function in uncertainty and disorder. If there is a single unifying thread to this discussion, it is the importance of building and developing leaders around adaptation, with lots of preparation and a focus on the selection and preparation of people with the passion, traits and attributes to teach as part of an ACM.

Teachers of adaptability

The role of teachers and their methods are different in an ACM than in the Army's traditional teaching model. Learning through many scenarios relies on a teacher's ability to introduce increasingly difficult unit tasks in the development of adaptive leaders. The program should constantly expose students to individual and collective tasks that they have never seen. Teachers should not get "wrapped around the task," but introduce and show students how the task fits into solving the larger problem. A better term would be to say students become "familiar" with most tasks instead of spending an incredible amount of time becoming "trained" (qualified) in any particular one.

The burden of imparting adaptability on students is with great teachers. Individuals that qualify for these key roles in an ACM are coined the teachers of adaptability (TA). They are constantly updating and preparing new challenges to their students through a rigorous study of the latest lessons as it is applies to the profession of arms. Teaching cognitive skills involves exposure to new ideas, encouragement to experiment with theories concerning what works and does not work, and the ability to learn, evaluate and assess. An ACM sets the conditions where evaluation occurs with the student through various mission scenarios, each with different conditions.

There is an art to teaching. In the Army, it requires an understanding of war, proficiency in the technical aspects of the profession of arms, good leadership, imagination and patience. There is no room for big egos in a classroom. With these ingredients, the teacher of adaptability will find many ways to utilize tasks to employ the teach-facilitate-mentor approach. The goal of a true teacher is to prepare students to be better problem solvers than the teacher.

The key to the ACM is that individuals must know how to teach, facilitate, mentor and evaluate adaptability. How the Army certifies the leaders it chooses to teach these courses is critical to the success of the ACM. This goes far beyond today's demand that instructors must master certain tasks or win certification as instructors by passing an online course consisting of multiple-choice questions.

Certainly teachers must understand individual tasks, but their knowledge cannot comprise only the ability to reinforce memorization of how to perform a certain task. Teachers of adaptability must understand the threads of knowledge that allow a combat leader to choose the appropriate number and type of tasks, how to combine these individual tasks as part of more complex task in order to solve the challenges that they will encounter in a 4GW environment.

More difficult, instructors must understand theories, and how to experiment to solve unknown or unfamiliar problems that might arise in the classroom or on the battlefield.

With these general insights about the nature of an ACM teacher, the next step is defining the selection and certification of teachers of adaptability.[162] Currently, the Army's Instructor Training Course (AITC), which certifies many of the Army's instructors, is dominated by a linear format which includes "how to" briefings on putting together lesson plans, schedules and calendars, all of which are focused on task proficiency. Selection of individuals to be Army instructors is usually based on the need to fill a slot, which in today's personnel system, are not considered career enhancing. The ACM will be limited if the personnel system fails to provide the necessary resources for leader-centric courses, including the best and brightest individuals for instructors.[163]

Certification for an ACM begins with the selection, and then the education, and finally the certification of those individuals who initially demonstrate the potential to teach adaptability. First of all, the Army as a learning organization needs to rank the importance of teaching at an ACM as second only to commanding or leading soldiers. The feeling among Army leaders should become, "if [I am] not leading or commanding troops, then teaching at an ACM is the next best option." Becoming and being a teacher of adaptability does not come from a career need, but from a burning desire to teach and develop future leaders.[164]

The Army should then select potential TAs based on recommendations from a soldier's chain of command and mentors. The evaluation reports of soldiers should also mention the traits and attributes mentioned in the beginning paragraphs of this section. In addition to the wishes of the individuals and recommendations of others, there could also be a competitive entry examination or an interview process wherein current TAs can further screen for the right teachers. Just because the candidate is selected to attend ACM certification does not automatically qualify them to teach in an ACM.

Those chosen to attend the ACM must be prepared to erase their memory. That is, they must unlearn how they themselves were trained in their careers. This will be a challenge to establish: preparing these newcomers to teach adaptability must occur within a positive and encouraging environment. Those preparing people to teach adaptability should impress upon them that the new methodology will come as a great shock, but that success will bring significant rewards – such as knowing that in turn their students will become well prepared for the most challenging endeavor, leading other soldiers in war.[165]

TA candidates attending the ACM certification course will encounter a course similar to the one that they will teach if they are certified as a TA. Learning for adaptation begins in the preparation prior to arrival to the course: students should be given minimal instruction but expected to have administrative requirements completed prior to their arrival. Web pages should provide them with necessary materials, but the student should be forced to do the work and complete the tasks on their own. Then, upon arrival on the first day, candidates should be put in positions where they have to teach to their peers. Intermittent between their stints as teachers, students will be taught by teachers of adaptability or "Jedi Knights"[166] – those who possess the most profound commitment and astute mind – on how to teach, infuse enthusiasm and relate the importance and development of implicit communication.

As candidates proceed through certification, they should be introduced to the ACM principles by experiencing them first hand, and then encouraged to discuss their value during an AAR. TA candidates should be constantly thrown into leading and teaching classes and observing other students conducting training. They should participate in AARs where current TAs introduce facilitation techniques such as active listening, the art of asking questions, teaching to the objective, and how to brief instructions. Teachers of adaptability may highlight these techniques by demonstrating how to do them correctly or incorrectly while the students critique the teacher's demonstration.

After the exposure to teaching adaptability in the classroom, students should be introduced to the scenarios and how to develop scenarios, as well as to the tools used to deliver scenarios through the experience of using case study method, tactical decision games or free play force-on-force exercises. All scenarios should conclude with a group AAR exercise, evaluating the candidate that facilitated the scenario, and finally the observing cadre should counsel the candidate on their performance through a questioning process. The TA should not provide answers during the counseling session, but merely provoke thought.

The students come to understand the nature of the feedback loop after going through several scenarios, AARs and counseling sessions. While the AAR can revolve around the performance of students in the scenario, students begin to grasp that the focus of feedback is not on whether decisions made during scenarios were good or bad. The key to feedback is that students come to understand the process, i.e., why and how the decision was made. Furthermore, students demonstrate in front of a TA that they can also facilitate an AAR and impart this process on their fellow students.

An ACM certification course should conclude with current TAs evaluating each student in his or her conduct of a scenario using a TDG. Each student should be given a scenario that they have not seen before, with little time to prepare. Then the student should demonstrate their ability to teach, facilitate, mentor and evaluate adaptability while conducting the scenario. The class will be composed of other TA candidates with one of the current TAs serving as an evaluated student (the student who will present their solution to the problem in the scenario). The scenario concludes with an AAR, followed by a TA candidate facilitating a discussion wherein the TA acting as the student will be questioned about his performance by the TA candidate.

Some candidates will pass this evaluation, and will move on to be certified as TAs, and others will not. Those candidates who do not attain the status of TA, return to their units with valuable skills they can apply to their current leadership roles, and at a later date may apply to return to the ACM certification course.

Even if the ACM is accepted as the new professional educational model for instilling adaptability in future Army leaders, it will fail if it is not resourced to attract not only talent, but those who want to teach. On the other hand, it is also unrealistic, with today's demands for good leaders and quality soldiers, to expect an ACM to get all the talent from the field. With this in mind there are a couple of ways the Army can ensure the ACM has quality teachers.

First, not every cadre member that occupies the traditional role of tactical officer (TAC) at a leader-centric course that uses the ACM needs to be certified. The Army can focus limited resources on preparing and certifying selected individuals who then take their abilities and skills, and occupy positions where they not only teach, but oversee other cadre members who are not qualified.

Second, the Army can compensate for shortfalls by the establishment of visiting teaching fellowships. These fellowships could be offered to civilians, as well as retirees that have already won awards and demonstrated their ability to teach. They would still have to be certified to teach at the ACM, but this would ensure the continuous flow of new ideas into and out of those leader-centric courses. If the ACM is to grow and harvest the adaptive leaders the Army will need to win in 4GW, then it must engender its cadre without stagnation.

Teaching in an ACM

Teaching in an ACM is mastering the art of facilitating. Facilitating or coaching means understanding and using different techniques: asking questions, using sarcasm and stepping in at the appropriate time and place with encouragement to continually rethink what they are doing, without being demeaning. Teaching in the ACM avoids, unless it is absolutely necessary, giving the student answers.

When the TA is acting as a coach it's possible to see another example of the art of facilitation. At appropriate times during a briefing, a TA can interject reality into a student's proposed solutions. The instructor may comment with phrases like "that's not possible," or "in reality this is what 'x' can do for you in that type of terrain." Or, the instructor can ask probing, Socratic questions such as, "Does your course of action coincide with the spirit of the commander's intent?" Or, "What caused you to change the mission you were given?" These repeated sessions aim at building character, adaptability, and intuition over time, through constant 360 degree assessments, feedback, mentoring and coaching. "Professionals have coaches. Amateurs do not."[167] In other words, those students aspiring to be professional officers should be coached in a way that teaches them how to think. Coaching does not involve giving them the answers. Coaching is the art of guiding the student toward the answer on his or her own, so it becomes embedded. This is education and not training. Teachers of adaptability are professionals, and coaches are indeed needed and appropriate. Beyond merely talking about it, effective coaching must be made a cultural cornerstone and practical reality of a course that teaches adaptability.

As Col. Jon Moilanen observed in a recent *Military Review* article:

Leaders mentoring leaders in a clearly defined manner, and complementary coaching of soldiers and teams, reinforces learning and motivation to adapt. Direct and recurring advice and counsel among leaders reinforces adaptive behaviors. Coaching has been demonstrated to contribute quantifiably to organizational productivity (up 53 percent), retention (up 39 percent), and job satisfaction (up 61 percent) according to 100 executives from Fortune 1000 companies.[168]

The major benefit of this type of education is that students can experience situations that are either hard to enact in actual training or too expensive to enact in the field or as a computer simulation (war games). Student leaders can go over literally hundreds of scenarios without ever leaving the classroom. At the same time, all types of training, from physical exercises to field exercises, can be facilitated with scenarios. Scenarios establish a solid foundation to understand decision-making prior to moving into the field and where repeated trials can be much more costly. Obviously, scenarios are not a substitute for free-play, force-on-force exercises, but they do make the time and expense in the latter more valuable.

The course environment of an ACM must be one that treats, relies and trusts its teachers as professionals. It is imperative in teaching adaptive learning to treat students – whether cadets or lieutenants – with respect, while strongly challenging the students to think for themselves. TAs know that they are teaching correctly if they are initially unpopular with their students, especially with younger students where society has taught them what to think in providing road maps in everything they do with safety nets that prevent them from failing.

The ACM teaching approach forces students to work hard to find answers. Then, they work even harder to self assess their performance in scenarios. Good TAs will constantly test their students, and respond to their questions with questions. Such a philosophy will quickly define the teaching environment. This approach will end trivial and insignificant aspects of current Army education, such as signing in and out, drill and ceremony, or marching students to an event in formation, while both training and educating. These methods also apply stresses and challenges to students without using the "rabid dog" approach (i.e. yelling).[169]

In the latter context, task training and leader development become one. Any training task should be seen as a vehicle to teach adaptability. Striking a balance between training conducted through task performance and education of adaptability is important. The accomplishment of the task alone is not as important as the environment that is used to create it, while the teacher facilitates learning. Given the Army's longstanding emphasis on skill mastery through competency-based education, the need for this innovation is hard to instill.

The students in a class might be using the same tasks and mission, but the teacher has to have the ability to change conditions. The teacher should continually revisit the progress of each student daily to evolve his or her lesson plans. This leads to constant AARs, and mentoring and counseling of individuals. The TAs use several methods to impart knowledge, and this includes the use of changing conditions of the situation while the students execute the scenario, the use of time, and the art of asking questions.

In changing the conditions of the scenario, the TA can create conflict between what students are ordered to do, and what is really going on. Instructors can also issue vague operation orders (OPORDs). This forces students to make assumptions or educated guesses. For instance, as a teacher observes a student leader and his subordinates studying and beginning to solve a given problem, he can facilitate by "plugging in bits of knowledge" to encourage students to ask questions.

Time is another factor teachers use to induce stress and enable adaptability. Teachers should time scenarios. When time is up, the student presents his or her solution. Peers then evaluate the student's decision-making ability, not how he or she accomplished the specific tasks and mission. If the student did not accomplish the mission goals, the peer group and student leader should discuss why they did not.[170] Limiting time also goes hand-in-hand with another stress induced approach: teaching students how to ask questions.

Telling students "there are no dumb questions" is counterproductive to teaching them how to think for themselves. Allowing them to ask dumb questions only reinforces bad habits such as not listening attentively when orders or guidance is given. In the real world, there is not much time for extensive follow-up questions over the tactical radio. Everything falls back to teaching the student how to deal with the stress of combat in the shortest amount of time.

Teachers must encourage students to seek more knowledge when they ask pertinent questions. The teacher will do this through the student brief-back of the proposed solution. Students should offer a solution to the TDG to their peers, who in turn should evaluate that student's decision. In this case, the instructor is there to guide and facilitate the discussion and to force the student to seek more answers (but with the condition that they should not provide the answers). Students should seek more knowledge, either in the syllabus or verbally from the instructor on their own time.

With vast preparation required, the learning organization strives to keep TAs in one of three states when "on duty": first, they will be teaching or facilitating, either in the classroom or in a training environment; second, they will be preparing for their next lesson or scenario; and finally, they will be evaluating student adaptability, which should always be accompanied by the provision of mentorship and either verbal or written feedback. The POI of the adaptive leader course puts more responsibility on the shoulders of both teacher and student to manage their time.

Teaching and coaching relies on the art of facilitating. Teachers and coaches facilitate by knowing the right time and place to say something that urges the student forward. They say just enough to leave the student to think about what they are doing, and figure out the solution.

Scenario and case study education[171]

A new leader paradigm will permit building richer and deeper understanding of the self and alternative approaches to problem solving that will enhance one's own ability to make good decisions. The Army's current and future operating environments demand that the emphasis from the outset in developing adaptability must be on growing by "learning-to-learn," not the mere ability to memorize information.

In the ACM, teaching is non-traditional with little reliance on podium lecture or the use of Power Point classes. The POI is experiential and revolves around scenarios. The process of learning through scenarios that grow in complexity requires the use of complex unit tasks in the development of adaptive leaders. Scenarios constantly expose and familiarize students with individual and collective tasks that they may have never seen before. Students are not "wrapped around the task," but instead encouraged to see how the task fits into solving the larger problem. Students become familiar with the task while participating in a scenario.

Students are always in a situation conducive to the development of personal initiative and adaptability. Everyone takes an active role in the course. This may consist of learning how to evaluate students during scenarios through other students' presentations, the observation of movie clips where adaptability was or was not demonstrated, evaluating other students from within a group, briefing solutions to the class or their group, or assuming a role during one of many exercises. This serves two objectives first it demonstrates experiential learning and second, it keeps students actively engaged.

Scenario based education should center on situations – both tactical and non-tactical – through an array of different tools to create the correct conditions in which the student can learn adaptability. Scenario-based education emphasizes one or more of the traits of adaptability as they were discussed in the beginning of chapter 1.

The teacher must thoroughly understand each aspect of adaptability in order to pass it on to students, both real world applications of adaptability as well as theory. Some aspects that are associated with adaptability include:

- Cognitive ability;[172]
- Problem-solving skills;[173] and
- Metacognitive skills; these comprise the ability to critically assess your own thoughts, always questioning, "Have I thought about this or that?" As well as looking from the outside in and saying, "What consequences does my decision have?"

Think of scenarios as "guideline-" and "principle-based" lesson plans that are templates the TA builds to teach students the aspects of adaptability. In the POI, responsibility for the improvement of training plans centers around a teacher's scenario development. It is not left to combat developers or academic committees.

TAs develop and evolve their scenarios for their students, while coming together during planning sessions to coordinate the next phase of leader development and to determine scenarios and the timing for events that involve larger units than individual classes and more resources. Scenarios are used to expose students to many different experiences in order to build and nurture intuition.

The purpose of the scenario-based education concept is to provide opportunities for each student to gain experience. Through multiple types of participation, either as a leader or team member, students receive breadth of experience and skills in decision-making to meet a specific set of circumstances. It is important to note that the teacher must also prepare to teach lessons from errors the students made in the execution of their plan.

Scenario-based education used with the proper tools provides students with supplemental information so that they can rely on experience when a new situation presents itself. Even so, these scenarios and the prescribed teaching approaches in this monograph are not substitutes for actual real-world experiences. Scenario-based concepts benefit student leaders by:

- Improving their pattern recognition skills;
- Allowing them to exercise the decision-making process;
- Improving and practicing their communication skills;
- Increasing their leadership potential; and
- Building character.

Scenarios to enable these skills come in many shapes and sizes; that is where the instructor's selection of a specific tool to deliver the scenario-based education is critically important. There are three other factors that must work together to produce learning synergy and successful scenario-based education. They are:

- The way that an instructor facilitates;
- The ability of students to understand what is being taught (material should be presented in a context the students can relate to – another skill of good teachers); and
- The instructor's capacity for mentorship (either individually or in a group through an after-action review).

Scenario packets integrate the required skills of adaptive leaders, to be practiced and evaluated in the course of a seminar discussion or exercise. While in some respects scenarios are built to be accomplished by a team, they should ideally be integrated seamlessly into the conduct of regular classroom instruction. In addition, principle-based lesson plans should include a history lesson that compels students to consider multiple perspectives. Some other aspects of scenario packets in an ACM:

- A tactical planning exercise that compels students to visualize plans that might accomplish an objective;
- A leadership lesson that may compel students to challenge their own biases; and

- If a student identifies a skill and wants to discuss it, that is encouraged.

Also, every scenario:

- Offers opportunities to practice leadership and decision-making, as well as to evolve adaptability; and
- Lets the learning objectives, not resources, drive the event.

Also, time is set aside for:

- Instructor preparation;
- Student opportunities to seek answers, or prepare for the next mission; and
- Observation of what students do when nothing else is required.

Teachers should continue to adjust scenarios through "lessons learned" and student feedback from previous classes. The goal is to create better and more efficient ways to nurture students into becoming adaptive leaders. All parts of the "learning organization" should contribute action and feedback – its "command and control" – through overall cooperation. The development of adaptive leaders is fundamentally an activity of reciprocal influence involving give-and-take among all parts, from top to bottom and from side to side.

Scenario packets should include descriptions of possible scenarios that the instructor can select or modify to teach aspects of adaptability. Each packet should begin with a historical case study followed by lessons learned. Scenario packets typically suggest past and possible student solutions, while also listing the strengths and weaknesses of each of the "tools" that the TA might use to deliver the scenario, ranging from a small group symposium, to the use of a sand table, to possibly a MOUT site battle with paint guns (always conducted as free play, force-on-force exercises).

The scenario packet should also include a list of all tasks the student may employ in tackling the scenario's problem, as well as a supporting annex that lays out the standards of that task. As a student's development continues, the instructor can pick tools and scenarios that are needed to provide the student with the experiences he needs to develop adaptability. The TA should base this on an assessment of the student and on what resources are available.[174]

Each TA can develop scenario packets based on his or her own experiences and key events in the course. These are points in which instructors assess the progress of their students and provide them feedback in order to make improvements. It does no good to give a very complex scenario if the student does not have the abilities or understanding of adaptability to attempt to solve the problem presented in a scenario, so in turn it assists the teacher with the evolution of the curriculum based on the evolution of the student.[175]

The TA can change the scenario cases based on what the students achieve as well as the level of proficiency of a student unit. While the teachers want students to "experience the thing before they try to give it a name," the teachers also want to give students problems that they can manage. This means that there should be some reasonable chance for them to solve a scenario, but only with a degree of stress. By exposing the students to overly complex problems, teachers may discourage them early on from taking risks and thinking boldly about their solutions.[176]

On the other hand, whenever possible, the teacher should use scenarios that place selected students three levels of command above their own. This assists teachers with two important tasks:

> • Observing what the student would do when presented with a complex problem involving a chain of command. Teachers should not be concerned with the student's ability to repeat information already given to him – what he knows – but rather, the student's willingness to use different types of information to solve the problem.

- Placing the student in a command level to be able to understand the place of their unit in the context of larger unit operations. It is not seeking to make them "experts" in higher-level operations, but to familiarize them with what goes on above their own level, and then giving their interpretation back to their peers. In essence, this "raises the bar," challenging selected students whose abilities require more difficult problem solving.[177]

Following each scenario, the instructor must sit down with the leader and his or her team, both together and separately, and go over what they have learned. With the individual, it should be similar to counseling. With a team, this can resemble the existing Army after action review process. Also, due to the Army's adherence to a "zero-defects" mentality, students will often use caution when admitting to their mistakes or allowing others to criticize them. The AAR can turn into a session of "who shot who" if not properly facilitated by the teacher.

Some people recommend a "pre-mortem" to the AAR. The pre-mortem should occur before the scenario is finished or before any presentation of solutions by students. In the pre-mortem exercise, the teacher tells his students to imagine that the situation has ended in failure. The teacher then facilitates the students through all the things that could have gone wrong with the scenario.[178]

Scenario delivery tools

Scenarios that deal with adaptability are situational-based events that require the individual to exercise mental agility to meet the demands of the situational stimuli as he or she implements a problem-solving solution. First, the TA can use the case study approach with their students as introduced in the last section, or based on an assessment of the students, the TA may decide to use the other two significant aspects of the adaptive course model POI:

(1) Tactical decision games (TDG) are one of the best ways to develop decision-making skills with little cost, but the teacher must know how to facilitate a TDG or the wrong lessons are taught. TDGs are also referred to as decision-making games (DMG)[179] by the Army Research Institute, which describes DMGs as:

low-fidelity, paper-and-pencil simulations of incidents that might occur in battlefield environments. A DMG presents a dilemma with high levels of uncertainty. Each participant has a limited amount of time to consider how he would react, which adds time pressure to the exercise. DMGs are intended to provide low-cost experiential training, and to allow practice in rapid decision-making. They also provide a context for teaching and practicing other exercises.[180]

TDGs put demands on teachers as well as the students

John Schmitt, who wrote a handbook on how to use TDGs called *Mastering Tactics*, describes how a TDG is used by a teacher and played by a student:

Playing a [tactical decision game] is very simple. Putting yourself [the teacher] in the role the commander, you read the situation [to the student]; within an established time limit so you decide what plan to adopt and communicate that plan in a form of the orders you [the student] would issue to your unit if the situation were for real. You provide an overlay of your plan. Then, and this is an important part of the process, you explain the plan as a means of analyzing why you did what you did.[181]

TDGs are common to a wide array of specialties, nationally and internationally. Teachers should introduce students to TDGs with problems they are not familiar with, such as combat troops doing non-combat TDGs, and just the opposite for support personnel. Particular courses or units may develop different operating procedures, but it is inadvisable to argue about specific procedural points. There will be plenty of time for that during the student debrief.[182]

TDGs do not have to be tactical. Other types of games exist: for example, the Los Angeles, California Fire Department has developed tactical decision games. Even the U.S. Army Chaplain Corps has developed its own games to deal with different scenarios that chaplains may experience.[183] Instructors of other Army leader programs have also developed very good games as tools to teach adaptability.

For example, Maj. [Ltc.] Philip Peck, a cadre at Boston University Army ROTC, uses what he calls leadership development exercises (LDEs) with his students. These provide a practical application for leadership development with little overhead. Peck can use the few resources that exist in the woods or around a field or parking lot in his problems. Each scenario in Peck's exercise program provides problem-solving tasks and situations that the cadets will have to address using an aspect of the U.S. Army troop-leading procedures as an appropriate tool in solving the problem at hand, and not as an end state. They have time constraints and problem-solving tasks that provide for stressful decision-making. Some situations Peck presents do not have easily identifiable answers.[184]

In whatever form a TDG is delivered, the TA should always encourage the student to treat the situation as if he or she were living it. In many of the scenario events, the student has literally fractions of a second to react, and allowing each one to ponder the situation for hours reduces the benefits of the exercise. Spontaneity is the key. Teachers must tell the student leader that the first reaction is probably the best one. Again, this is a good tool to build character, especially when a student's course of action is being attacked by the rest of the class.

After the TDG is conducted, the TA should require the student to defend his or her course of action. No matter what the course of action, if the student thinks he or she is right, the teachers must require him or her to defend it. Teachers need to divorce themselves from their egos in order to support a student's decision, even if that decision contradicts the solution the teacher developed before presenting the TDG to the class. The teachers must ask as they listen and guide the cadet during the briefing: is the student's course of action sound?[185]

Another method that can be used during a TDG is to have students imagine that they are giving orders to their unit, or explaining their actions to their battalion commander. One good approach is for the teacher to read scenarios to the students while the student leaders keep their eyes closed – that is, without the benefit of taking notes. In single-person scenarios, teachers can have the student leader describe the techniques that he or she plans to use, the rationale for that decision, and the follow-ups he or she plans to perform.[186]

In team scenarios, students describe what each student leader is doing and why, and spell out their actions and reactions. When placed under a time constraint, this approach teaches the student leaders how to time-manage, assign and communicate tasks and prioritize tasks. It becomes an effective tool to lead subordinates in planning and executing a mission with the severe time constraints commonly found on today's battlefield.

The TA can also add stress in other ways during the TDG. Some examples are: playing a war movie or loud music in the background; opening the windows and letting in the cold air during the winter; and keeping a radio speaker turned on in the classroom, continually updating the enemy and friendly situation. Teachers should feel free to devise any other form of distraction to approximate what the would-be leaders would feel in the heat of an actual battle.

There are no "right" answers. All responses have some benefit and will highlight the students' perceptions of the problem. There is nothing to stop cadets from coming up with more than one response. Recognizing, however, that there are many ways to approach a problem, cadre should not limit the cadets to a single pass-or-fail solution. This can be hard when using the TDG to evaluate decision-making ability during an examination, but it can be done.

The teacher can change or adjust all of these based on what he wants to achieve and the level of proficiency of the student or the class. As noted earlier, while teachers want students to have experiences before they try to name it, teachers also want to give them problems they can manage or that the students have a chance to solve. TDGs also provide excellent introduction to the next POI curriculum pillar:[187]

(2) Free play, force-on-force field exercises. These can range from team-versus-team exercises using paintball guns in nothing larger than a room-clearing exercise or small wooded lot, or large platoon or company-sized exercises in the field.

Free play force-on-force exercises are the most complex and usually the most resource driven aspect of the POI. Free play force-on-force exercises can be conducted by actual freethinking opponents, such as one student unit portraying U.S. forces, while the other plays the role of the insurgent forces. Or the exercise can be conducted also using opposing sides, but executed using computer simulation without leaving a building. Force-on-force, free play exercises should also occur at different levels of a leader's development, and the exercises will lends themselves well to higher levels of student education.

Using "in the field" exercises at the tactical level will likely necessitate the use of several TAs and non-TA cadre, who are able to assist with the conduct of the scenario. Another misplaced belief by today's culture is that these exercises should be a "free for all," with little or no control. Again, to produce the best results, much preparation should be done including the creation of realistic missions and orders to give to the opposing sides in a scenario. Then, after students decide what they are going to do, what their objectives will be, and what resources they will need, TAs and supporting cadre should conduct a "walk through" of the exercise to see if it makes sense as it is written, or whether it should be modified in order to meet learning objectives, and whether it's possible to conduct the scenario within a reasonable timeframe.

The walk through should be conducted as if students are taking the courses of action they would select during the scenario. The TAs and other cadre should use radios during the walk through as well as during actual execution in order to pass along observations from the opposing side, so the TA can use the information during the AAR, or to help facilitate the exercise. This also allows the TA to anticipate contact with the opposing side, to mentally prepare and war game what the student leader might do, and afterwards, what the student might have done prior to and during the contact – be it lethal or non-lethal. A time rehearsal should always build in the time it takes to conduct the AAR, as well as preparation times for movement and equipment, such as simulation calibration to real weapons. If these activities are not thought through and planned, and then executed to standard, then the actual event will turn into "Cowboys and Indians" and in turn degrade any development of adaptability.

While the force-on-force, free play exercise is seen as a course's or unit's premier event, there are also other ways the TA can deliver or introduce scenarios. Other tools to deliver a scenario include:

- Terrain board exercises (TBE), which aid teachers by showing at the micro level how terrain and weather affects a scenario. A TBE is a three-dimensional terrain model that uses various props to represent terrain, assets and liabilities. A scenario is applied once the terrain board exercise is prepared. The scenario lists assets, or factors, such as weather and materials (weapons and vehicles) that the student can use to develop a solution or optimize performance in some manner. Liabilities may include factors that invite unrealistic courses of action.

For example, a common error in combat is the miscalculation of speed and distance. Sometimes students project a solution that is impossible to implement because they ask one of their elements to move too far and too fast through terrain that would inhibit or slow even the best-trained units. The teacher must be prepared to challenge students' proposed actions, and facilitate a discussion that makes students rethink their judgments. The students should show confidence in their chosen course of action, and be able to explain how he or she arrived at the solution.

A terrain board is a good way to employ a TDG, but another use of a terrain board is in phase one or classroom preparatory work for a "staff ride," as well as during the AARs after the staff ride, to compare and contrast with what the participants observed. This can take the form of:

- A "listening exercise" where the teacher translates instructions from paper into an oral presentation to the students, followed by the students having a limited time to write the instructions down and give them back to the instructor;
- Virtual computer-based war games where several students execute the same scenario of a game, and then discuss whether they were able to solve it;[188] and

• Staff rides, in which cadre take the students to a battlefield following an introductory, preparatory phase in the classroom. The actual visit is not a tour, but rather, an interactive experience where students role play one of the battle's leaders, briefing his or her peers, as well as their teachers, on the perspective of that leader. The staff ride concludes with an AAR on what the students learned. However, the staff ride in an ALC is not the one currently practiced by some units in the U.S. Army where it becomes a staff tour.

A staff ride of an ALC employs an experiential training program that uses metaphorical exercises to teach leadership, teamwork and many other aspects of command and organizational effectiveness. Students learn work-related lessons while walking the very fields that Robert E. Lee and George Meade fought over. In the subcategory of military metaphors, battlefield and campaign staff rides place students in leadership roles, representing all levels of command to conduct decision-making and team-building sessions.

Leader Evaluation System (LES)

The ACM curriculum and Leader Evaluation System (LES) will use two criteria to judge whether students did well: the timelessness of their decisions, and their own justification for it. The first criterion will impress on the student the need to act quickly, while the second requires the student to reflect on their actions and gain insights into their own thought process. Since the student has to justify their decision in their own mind before implementing it, imprudent decisions and rash actions will be less likely.

During their coursework, what the student decides to do will be relatively unimportant. The emphasis will be on the effect of the students' actions overall, not on the method they may have chosen. The ACM will create a learning environment where there will be no formulas, or processes to achieve optimum solutions. This environment will solicit creative solutions.

The LES is based on the idea that undue criticism, after the fact, of a soldier on the scene – who will be in a confused, dangerous, and pressured situation and who has the best command of immediate information – is unwarranted. Anything beyond a constructive critique will only destroy the student leader's willingness to act and might even lead them to withhold adverse information or provide falsely optimistic reports simply to avoid a less than perfect evaluation report. An ACM will recognize there is little in adaptability that is systematic and will make allowance for it.

The heart and soul of adaptability – a theme throughout an ACM – will be the desired result, not the way the result is achieved. Teachers of adaptability should reject any attempt to control the type of action initiated during a mission because it is counter-productive. The ACM should instead concentrate on instilling in students the will to act, as they deem appropriate in their situations to attain a desired result.

The LES should be a "double loop" system defined as "the knowledge of several different perspectives that forces the organization to clarify differences in assumptions across frameworks, rather than implicitly assuming a given set."[189]

Whether on an exam employing TDGs, or during training, teachers should use multiple tools to give students continual and detailed evaluations that will allow the cadet to evolve, improve, and prepare for the graded field evaluations. During these tests, students will be evaluated on their ability to lead, demonstrate adaptability and make intuitive decisions under varied conditions. Evaluation criteria should consider the following questions:

1. First and foremost, did the student make a decision?
2. If so, did the student effectively communicate it to subordinates?
3. Was the decision made in support of the commander's intent (long-term contract), and mission (short-term contract)?

4. If not, was the student's solution based on changing conditions that made it a viable decision, even if it violated the original mission order, but nevertheless supported the commander's intent?

"Guiding actions" intertwine with the Army's core values when evaluating a student's leadership performance and potential. The stakes are high, as retired Lt. Gen. Walt Ulmer described it: "The Army needs to broaden its understanding of successful leadership from one that focuses almost entirely upon mission accomplishment; to one that includes long-term organizational health of the unit and its personnel alongside of mission accomplishment."[190]

In other words, the Army's current culture evaluates successful performance by determining whether a leader accomplished a specific mission. The focus is on the "bottom line." However, this method is shortsighted, and in the current leader paradigm, it can produce "performers" rather than leaders.

Measuring a student's potential, on the other hand, allows for an assessment that incorporates a student's ability to develop teams as well as subordinates, even in a classroom setting. This method can also include measurements of a student's loyalty, initiative and risk-taking.

To create problems that will properly demonstrate a student's potential, scenarios must be used that encourage students in subordinate roles to take risks in accomplishing their mission. In the AAR, the student commander should praise good performance of his peers (in the subordinate role), while accepting responsibility for their failure. The idea is that students will eventually emulate this behavior over time, and begin to realize their potential.[191]

Assessments should involve more than just cadre and student observations of a cadet's level of adaptability. Performance evaluations also occur in the classroom.

However, this does not imply that the use of traditional, Industrial Age testing techniques should be continued, because those techniques only reinforce rote memorization. These negative techniques include "true or false" questioning, "fill-in the blank" or "multiple-choice" examinations. However, cadres like to save time by using these linear evaluation techniques. They also provide quick feedback to the tested student, the cadre, and the chain of command when utilized for reports and Power Point slides. But these teaching techniques cheat the student because they focus on short-term results.

Since "knowledge" and "social judgment" are also part of the traits of adaptability, continual observations and evaluations of how a leader chooses to communicate decisions to subordinates or to inform the chain of command must occur. If leaders do not communicate decisions effectively to their subordinates or units, it makes no difference whether they are decisive or timely. Thus, teachers should use essay-based evaluations in the classroom. The use of essays will require that teachers have a firm grasp on the English language, grammar and style, and essays will also take more time to evaluate, but in the end they will provide a much deeper sense of the students' educational progress.

What should teachers look for in evaluating student leaders? A teacher should look for leadership failures that suggest weak character. For instance, if a student changes his original decision in order to go along with the instructor-recommended solution, or if the student stays with a poor or out-of-date decision from higher authority simply because that is what "higher" told him to do, teachers should mark these traits as a failure. The worst thing a student could do is to make no decision at all.

Evaluations can be used to award and highlight superior performance. They are also used to serve as a record on which TAs might evaluate an individual's ability to become a leader. An effective organization should further reward students when they exceed the standards, while enforcing the standards themselves. Failure in timely enforcement of standards, that all students are required to follow, degrades the effectiveness of the organization. In warfare, it undermines trust and endangers soldiers' lives.

As stated above, inability to make any decision is a failure in a scenario using any tool. Another sign of failure on a scenario would be if a student changes his or her decision simply because the instructor challenged the student's choice during the course of briefing.

If that occurs, the student is demonstrating a common failing – the wish to go along with the instructor. Even if the instructor believes that the student's decision is a sound one, he may challenge or test the student's character in the face of adversity to see how much the student truly believes in him or herself. In the end, TDGs provide one of the best educational approaches for building a student's strength of character as well as cognitive abilities.

The bottom line is the need to develop teaching tools that help develop adaptability while staying away from the use of tools that involve more time and resources in procuring and operating, or that distract from the main objective. Maj. Frank Brewster of the U.S. Army describes his use of TDGs, or as he calls them, tactical decision exercises (TDE):

The TDE provides an effective mechanism for developing individual ability to make decisions under physical and mental stress. While TDEs are not the perfect substitute for actual training and experience, they do serve to sharpen individual intuitive decision-making ability. In today's military, constrained as it is by shrinking budgets, personnel shortages, and numerous missions, TDEs provide leaders at all levels an opportunity to hone decision-making skills during scenarios that place the student-leader in stressful situations. Recently, there has been a resurgence of the TDE variety of war games. Experiences in peace operations have rekindled interest in the merits of using these role-playing scenarios to develop decision-making skills.[192]

The Adaptive Course Model works!

In the end, scenario-based learning provides an educational approach for building a student's strength of character. Past curricula that dealt with leader development used process and task training to dictate to potential officers "what to think." Today, the Army is beginning to realize that the foundation of an effective future officer corps must begin early, and that to create leaders that are adaptable, they need to know "how to think" in order to develop intuition.

The ACM will hold to the first idea that every moment and event offers an opportunity to develop adaptability. Every action taken by a student in the classroom or in the field is important to the process of inculcating a preference for solutions. If a student errs while acting in good faith, they should not suffer anything more than corrective mentoring. Constructive critiques of solutions are the norm in an ACM, but more important in this model are the results of a student's action, and the reasons for taking that action. This will spread throughout the Army culture, once implemented by the ACM.

The role of mentoring and 360-degree assessments should be used to teach the student that their future actions will make a positive contribution to their unit's success, no matter what the mission.

ACM teachers will also place an emphasis on ensuring that students gain and then maintain an instinctive willingness to act. During numerous AAR and mentoring sessions – occurring during and after numerous scenarios under varied conditions – the teacher should analyze why the student acted as he did and the effect the student's action has on the overall operation.

Beyond decision-making in war, the use of the ACM model also has applications to the corporate world as well as any organization that needs leaders who are decisive and adaptable. Establishing a blend of instructional technologies is critical to promoting growth in cognitive and emotional skills, and consequently knowledge development.

Current Army instructional approaches lack opportunities for experiencing the emotional trauma of failing within a safe environment – something that is needed to promote maturity. The ACM permits building richer and deeper understandings of the self and alternative world views, an understanding of which will enrich one's own self-understanding. The Army's highly technical environment and its mission to fight uncertain and complex foes in the 21st century demands that the emphasis from the outset be on growing by "learning to learn," and not learning information alone.

Chapter 4
Conclusion: The Beginning

"Most Army schools open with the standard bromide: 'We are not going to teach you what to think … we are going to teach you how to think.' They rarely do. Critical thinking is both art and science. There are techniques to critical thinking, such as careful application of logic, or alternative application of deduction and induction. These techniques can be taught and learned."[193]
    Brig. Gen. David Fastabend and Robert Simpson

The strategic approach and tactical techniques inherent in 4GW will require major changes in the way the U.S. Army educates, employs, structures and trains its future forces and leaders. A good start is to broaden professional education – from initial-entry training to the top war-college level – to deal with the wide spectrum of issues that commanders will confront in 4GW. The Army must also understand that even in competent conventional warfare, 3GW, the Army builds trust on high levels of professionalism and unit cohesion. As one captain put it, leaders must be prepared to "group together from a new perspective a number of measures that have been used before but were viewed separately."[194]

Critically important to the institutionalization of adaptability in the Army will be superior military education and training. Not only will the Army need to produce leaders that possess adaptability, but the institutions tasked to develop leaders will need to become adaptive as well – to evolve as the future operating environment evolves. The ACM will provide principles that allow implementation of central ideas.

The Army's cultivation of adaptability requires a vast effort – from the "top-down" as well as "bottom-up." It is so central to the future of the Army that it applies to squad leaders as well as to the joint-force commander. The leaders of the future Army should have to make a truly gross error to create a negative blotch on their careers. Evaluations and performance reviews cannot continue to haunt adaptive leaders throughout their careers if they have only made an honest mistake.

Moving the Army toward a learning organization structure, where its institutions as well as its leaders are adaptive, will bring the collective creativity of the Army to bear in solving problems at the tactical, operational and strategic levels of war. The culture will become one that rewards leaders and soldiers who act, and penalizes the ones who do not. Today's culture needs to evolve so that the greater burden rests on all superior officers, who have to nurture – teach, trust, support and correct – the student who now enters the force with the ability to adapt.

The Army's future leaders will also have the responsibility to self-police their own ranks, particularly early on if they become TAs within an ACM. This makes evaluating, "racking and stacking" of graduates easier. It will also help determine early on who will have the character and traits to become an adaptive leader. The criteria should include observations of the student leaders in several scenarios. Before selecting or promoting subordinates, a TA should always be asked, "would I want this person to serve in my unit?" Throughout an ACM, a TA will instill in students the importance of accurate reporting and taking action when the situation demands it. The Army's culture of the future will not tolerate inaction. Indecisiveness or the inability to make a decision will become the culture's cardinal sin, not playing it safe.

Adaptability will become a product of the future Army; it will depend on what appears to be a relatively simple change in teaching technique in order to deal with the increasing complexities of war. The grasping, understanding and mastering of adaptability will come through rigorous education and tough training early on – quality, not quantity – to produce adaptive leaders. Leaders' ability to be adaptable will guide decisions on how to accomplish their missions, while also helping them to recognize and compensate for differences in the temperament and ability of other Army officers, NCOs and civilians through unit training and professional development. Adaptability will provide a stable support structure to infuse and sustain Army leaders' initiative in future operating environments.

Today's Army leadership must understand that by simply using the word "adaptability" in Power Point presentations, saying they are going to implement it, or repackaging curriculums and personnel policies to include rhetoric about adaptability, while leaving the substance unchanged, will not adequately prepare leaders to be adaptive. The entire Army must be prepared to support, nurture, and reinforce it.

This monograph presented a conflict between rhetoric and reality: the desire to evolve the culture of the Army so it can fight and win a 4GW conflict, and the reality of how hard it is going to be to achieve this by changing an Army culture founded in the Industrial Age. This tension will result in a short-term crisis where the Army may find its most promising junior leaders voting with their feet and leaving. Why? Because it is all too likely that these future leaders will discover that the Army leadership is ignoring them due to their low rank and grade, despite their abilities to think and act at higher levels of responsibility.

If this "trust problem" is fixed then the Army will find that it has also solved the larger problem. The Army will wind up retaining the "right" folks – those with a "calling to the service" who can prepare and lead the Army in the 21st century. Establishing an ACM and allowing it to continue to evolve into the future is the first step in changing Army culture to truly prepare the service to deal with the complex battlefield environment of the 21st century.

The Army is saying the right things regarding change, and it is beginning to execute ideas evolving from its rhetoric. Cultural change is generational and occurs with the understanding that "critical thinking is a learned behavior that is underpinned by education. The Army education system, moreover, can be our most effective lever of cultural change. Many of our most important cultural shifts can trace their origins to the schoolhouse. A thorough review of the institutional educational system is required to assess its effectiveness at engendering critical thinking."[195]

Acknowledgements

I would like to thank the late Air Force Col. John Boyd for his inspiration; Franklin C. Spinney and Bruce I. Gudmundsson for their mentorship; Lt. Col. Allen Gill, Majs. Marty Klein and Robert Goodfellow, and Sgt. 1st Class Jeffery Roper for their comradeship; and recognize the rest of the faculty and cadre, alumni (2000-2005) and cadets of Georgetown University's Army ROTC program for their insights and thoughts. Special thanks to Steven Stewart and Cols. George Reed and Chris Paparone, U.S. Army, for their continual insights; Maj. John F. Schmidt, USMCR, for sharing his concepts on teaching when I began the quest for better leader education; Lt. Col. Isaiah Wilson who shaped my thoughts alongside his own efforts to reform officer education; and to Marcus Corbin and Winslow Wheeler at CDI for their encouragement and insights. Finally, my wife Lorraine for her constant sacrifice of her time with me in pursuit of doing what is right.

Interested in applying what you have read?

Don Vandergriff's latest venture -Adaptive Leader LLC - introduces his ideas on creating and nurturing Adaptive Leadership to commercial, emergency services and other fields. Interested parties are invited to visit adaptive-leader.com for more information, or send an email to contactus@adaptive-leader.com.

About the Author

Maj. Donald E. Vandergriff, U.S. Army, retired on Aug. 30, 2005, following
24 years of active duty as an enlisted Marine and Army officer. He has served in numerous troop, staff and education assignments in the United States and overseas. Vandergriff was named ROTC instructor of the year 2002-2003 and the 3rd ROTC Brigade instructor of the year for 2003-2004. Vandergriff is a recognized authority on the U.S. Army personnel system, Army culture, leadership development, soldier training and, in the early 21st century, the emergence of asymmetric warfare, also known as 4th generation warfare (4GW). He has authored over 50 articles as well as numerous briefings and books.

The U.S. Army Training and Doctrine Command's Future Center – renamed in December 2005 as Army Capabilities Integration Center (ARCIC) – located at Fort Monroe, Va., hired Vandergriff to contribute toward the evolution of Army leader development programs and to recommend changes that will prepare the Army's leaders and soldiers for the future.

Vandergriff wrote this monograph in his free time during the final days of his assignment at Georgetown University Army ROTC. He has already shared its contents with the Army chain of command and other service agencies that deal with leader development.

Vandergriff and his wife, Lorraine, currently reside in Woodbridge, Va., with their numerous dogs and a cat.

Endnotes

1. Author e-mail correspondence with Army Chief of Staff Gen. Peter Schoomaker, "Adjustments to Transformation for a Better Army," Nov. 22, 2004.

2. I define 'holistic' as involving all the institutions that compose how the Army accesses its officers. In the context of the Army, holistic includes defining all the second and third-order effects that impact other institutions within the U.S. Army Training & Doctrine Command (TRADOC) and those commands under TRADOC, such as Accessions Command and Cadet Command, as well as Cadet Command's subordinate commands, its two regions, 14 brigades and 270 battalions.

3. I cannot begin to thank Sgt. 1st Class Jeffrey Roper. He is one of the finest non-commissioned officers I have had the honor to serve with. He is one of the best teachers I have ever witnessed. He always spoke to the cadets in a positive yet challenging way.

4. Millis, Walter, ed. American Military Thought. Indianapolis, Ind: Bobbs-Merrill Co. 1966. pp. 12-14; George Washington had proposed a federal Continental Militia, a small regular army and a military academy as the system best suited for defense. Again, in 1790, Secretary of War Henry Knox proposed a universal professional militia controlled by the federal government. Both moves died in Congress.

5. Wass de Czege, Col. Huba. "How to Change an Army." Military Review. Leavenworth, Kan.: U.S. Army Command and General Staff College. November 1984.

6. Schmitt, John F. "Command and (Out of) Control: The Military Implications of Complexity Theory." Complexity, Global Politics, and National Security. eds. David S. Alberts and Thomas J. Czerwinski. Washington, D.C.: National Defense University Press. 1998. There is another way to think about the differences between major power/3GW conflict and small/4GW conflicts. John Schmitt makes an important argument about the implications of small/4GW conflict in this chapter.

7. Ibid.

8. Ibid.

9. Minson, Jeff. "Strategies for Socialists? Foucault's Conception of Power." Towards a Critique of Foucault. ed. Gane, Mike. London: Routledge & Kegan. 1996. pp. 122.

10. Czerwinski, Thomas. Coping with the Bounds: Speculations on Non-linearity in Military Affairs. Washington, D.C.: National Defense University Press. 1998. Available at http://www.dodccrp.org/coptin.htm.

11. Coffman, Edward M. The Old Army: A Portrait of the American Army in Peacetime, 1784-1898. New York, NY: Oxford University Press. 1986. pp. 61-64 and 194-198. Also see, Elting, John R. American Army Life. New York, NY: Scribner's. 1982. pp. 55, 84. For information on a period of social reform between the Civil War and the Spanish-American War that precede Root, see Foner, Jack D. The United States Soldier between Two Wars: Army Life and Reforms, 1865-1898. New York, NY: Humanities Press. 1970. Foner discerns two distinct periods of reform, the first in the early 1880s and a second in the late 1880s and early 1890s. Spurred by the civil service reform movement of the early 1880s and later by what became the progressive movement, the Army secured numerous social reforms, all aimed at making service life more attractive for the enlisted soldier.

12. Discussions with Dr. Faris Kirkland, April 12 and May 8, 1998. Also see: Kirkland, Faris. "The Gap between Leadership Policy and Practice: A Historical Perspective." Parameters. Carlisle, Penn: U.S. Army War College. September 1990. pp. 54-55; Coffman. pp. 23-40, 101-103 & 176-180; Elting. pp. 38-45, 76-78; and Weigly, Russell F. "American Strategy from its Beginnings through the First World War." Makers of Modern Strategy from Machiavelli to the Nuclear Age. ed. Peter Parat. Princeton, N.J.: Princeton University Press. 1986. pp. 439-441. The Army reformers under Upton failed to reform West Point on the German model. In 1881, Gen. John Schofield resigned as superintendent citing political meddling when he tried to change the curriculum from an engineering focus to a military art focus. Gradually, some technical courses were replaced with more broad, liberal, and military art as in the German system. Several officers including William T. Sherman did see the failure of the Army's organization and policies during the Civil War. A small group of officers, called "Uptopians" after Gen. Emory Upton, attempted some type of reforms for three decades after the Civil War, and met largely with failure.

13. Lane, Jack C. Armed Progressive. San Rafael, Calif.: Presidio Press. 1978. pp. 150. Also see, Upton, Emory. The Armies of Asia and Europe. Washington, D.C.: U.S. Government Printing Office. 1878. pp. 219. Upton considered the U.S. Army experience as misguided and disastrous. He considered the overall performance of the U.S. Army in all previous wars as unprofessional and wasteful of lives. These results he attributed to ineffective policy regarding an amateur officer corps, a reliance on a militia system and faulty organization. It was General-in-Chief William T. Sherman who was behind sending Upton to Europe, specifically to study the Prussian Army, instead of sending the corrupt Belknap to Europe. Dickinson, John. The Building of an Army. New York, N.Y.: The Century Co. 1922. pp. 245-270. At the time, the officer corps was not professional. Examinations and efficiency reports were used, but nothing was done when officers failed them or received a bad report. Promotions, commissions, and appointments were more often based upon favoritism and political pull than merit. The most common argument in favor of the "up-or-out" promotion system is the experience during the Civil War and World War II, where hundreds of officers too old to perform in the field had to be replaced by younger and more vigorous officers. This argument ignores the fact that, unlike today, no mental and physical evaluations existed. Hammond, Paul Y. Organizing for Defense: The American Military Establishment in the Twentieth Century. Princeton, N.J.: Princeton University Press. 1961. p. 10. Hammond asserts that President William McKinley brought in Root "to clean up the mess" left by the Spanish-American War. Cosmas, Graham A. An Army for Empire: The United States Army in the Spanish-American War. Columbia, Mo.: University of Missouri Press. 1971. p. 311. Cosmas claims that "McKinley strove to organize the Army on the principles elaborated by Emory Upton." Bernard, Chester I. The Functions of the Executive. Cambridge, Mass.: Harvard University Press. 1938. p. 148.

14. Vandergriff, Donald. "Renaissance in the 1980s." Path to Victory: America's Army and the Revolution in Human Affairs. Novato, Calif.: Presidio Press. May 2002. This is a near exception to that statement. While great strides of improvement were made to doctrine, equipment, and personnel, it was not to the point where it aligned with the doctrine of Air Land Battle, specifically in regards to agility, initiative and decisiveness. Unit manning, called COHORT, was attempted, but was eliminated at the height of the 1990 Gulf War due to it being a smaller part of a larger individual-centric personnel system. Also the "up-or-out" promotion system negatively influenced all regulations and policies of personnel management.

15. For a good comparison of this ongoing trend, see: Elliot, J.H. The Count-Duke of Olivares: A Statesman in an Age of Decline. Hartford, Conn.: Yale University Press. February 1990.

16. Morrison, James L. "Military Education and Strategic Thought, 1846-1861." Against All Enemies: Interpretation of American Military History from Colonial Times to the Present. ed. Kenneth J. Hagan and William R. Roberts. New York: Greenwood Press. 1986. p. 105.

17. Morrison, p. 105.

18. Lt. Col. Chris Hughes' talk to Georgetown Corps of Cadets, April 15, 2005.

19. Jones, Col. Stephen. "Improving Accountability for Effective Command Climate: A Strategic Imperative." Strategic Studies Institute. Carlisle, Penn.: U.S. Army War College. September 2003. p. v.20 Fastabend, Brig. Gen. David A. and Simpson, Robert H. "Adapt or Die: The Imperative for a Culture of Innovation in the United States Army." Army Magazine. Association of the United States Army. November 2003.

21. Fastabend and Simpson, p. 6.

22. Snider, Don. "The U.S. Army as Profession." The Future of the Army Profession. ed. Lloyd J. Matthews, Don M. Snider and Gayle L. Watkins. New York: McGraw-Hill. 2002. pp. 10-11.

23. Steele, Dennis. "Commanders in Iraq, Some Lessons Learned." Army. Arlington, Va.: Association of the United States Army. June 2005. Available at http://www.ausa.org/armymagazine. Also, based on discussions with Lt. Col. Jim Chevallier, June 2005, as well as by e-mail.

24 . Wilcox, Greg and Richards, Chet. "4GW, OODA Loops, and Implications of the Iraqi Insurgency." Delivered at the 16th Strategy Conference, Army War College. Carlisle, Penn. April 12-14, 2005.

25. Becker, Capt. Jordan. Discussions with author on cadet and cadre survey.

26. One only has to go to the website of the Washington, D.C.-based think tank RAND to view their latest proposals as well as a wealth of articles. Also see, Killibrew, Col. Robert. "Winning Wars." Army. Arlington, Va.: Association of the United States Army. April 2005. Available at http://www.army.mil/professionalwriting/volumes/volume3/may_2005/5_05_2.html.

27. Vandergriff, Donald, et al. "Future of the U.S. Army." Presentation at the American Enterprise Institute, April 11, 2005. Transcript available at http://www.aei.org/events/f.video,eventID.1011,filter.all/event_detail.asp.

28. Wheeler, Winslow. The Wastrels of Defense: How Congress Sabotages U. S. Security. Annapolis, Md.: Naval Institute Press. 2004.

29. I am indebted to Maj. Isaiah Wilson, a professor in the sociology department of the U.S. Military Academy, for his insights on many editions of the draft study that preceded this manuscript.

30 . Reed, Col. George. "Toxic Leaders." Military Review. Fort Leavenworth, Kan.: U.S. Army Command and General Staff College Press. July-August 2004. Also attributed to author's discussion with Reed, April 14, 2005.

31 . Fastabend and Simpson, p. 6

32. Was de Czege, Brig. Gen. Huba. "Report of the Commandant's Special Review Team for Command and General Staff College Missions and Methods." Unpublished report, U.S. Army Combined Arms Center, Fort Leavenworth, Kan. Dated March 11, 2005.

33. Two books have been written on Col. John Boyd: Hammond, Grant. The Mind of War: John Boyd and American Security. Washington, D.C.: Smithsonian Books. 2001.; and Corum, Robert. Boyd: The Fighter Pilot Who Changed the Art of War. New York: Little, Brown, and Co. November 2002.

34. Briggs, John and Peat, F. David. Turbulent Mirror. New York: Harper and Row. 1989. Also, Van Creveld, Martin. Transformation of War. Cambridge: Harvard University Press. 1985.

35. Hays, S.P. "Introduction." Building the Organizational Society. ed. Israel, J. New York: Free Press. 1971. Also see, Hays, J.H., "The Evolution of Military Officer Personnel Management Policies: A Preliminary Study with Parallels from Industry." Santa Monica, Calif.: Rand. 1978.

36. Doughty, R. Seeds of Disaster: The Development of French Doctrine, 1919-1939. New York: Archon Books. 1986.

37. Swift, Maj. E. Field Orders, Messages and Reports. Washington, D.C.: Government

38. Printing Office Document UB283.A45. 1906. Stewart, S.R. "Leader Development Training Assessment of U.S. Army TRADOC Brigade Commanders." Washington, D.C.: U.S. ARI Research Report 1454.

38. Vandergriff, Donald E. "Raising the Bar: Creating Adaptive Leaders to Deal with the Changing Face of War." Unpublished study. Washington, D.C.: Georgetown University Army ROTC. June 2005. While conducting the study upon which this monograph is based, I learned that the ROTC POI places leadership training fourth in priority behind Cadet Mandatory Training, First Aid, and Operations and Tactics for pre-commissioning tasks to be taught to cadets. Cadet Command places greater emphasis on teaching the cadets how to become soldiers than how to become leaders of soldiers. The original study recommended that Cadet Command integrate leadership tasks and training to maximize instructor contact hours. The fact that ROTC institutions have limited opportunities to train supports the review of common skills tasks taught in the formal portion of ROTC training. Another finding of this study was that the current ROTC POI does not teach the leadership attributes currently listed in Field Manual 22-100. Of the 11 leadership pre-commissioning tasks taught, none of them informs the cadets about the leadership attributes listed in current doctrine. This is primarily due to the ROTC POI being published prior to the publishing date on FM 22-100.

39. E-mail communication with several junior officers – alumni from Georgetown Army ROTC, as well as many other officers including those who were commissioned from West Point as well as Officer Candidate School.

40. E-mail communication with Maj. Ike Wilson to author, March 30, 2005.

41. E-mail communication with Maj. Ike Wilson to author, Feb. 3, 2005.

42. Wilson, Maj. Isaiah. "The Beyond War Project: In Search of a Theory and Method of War for the Postmodern Age." West Point, NY: United States Military Academy. 2005.

43. Brownlee, Les and Schoomaker, Gen. Peter. "Serving a Nation at War: Toward a Campaign Quality Army with Joint and Expeditionary Qualities." Parameters. Carlisle, Penn.: The Army War College. p.18.

44. U.S. Army Accessions Command. "Basic Officer Leader Course Briefing." Fort Monroe, Va.: BOLC Task Force. Jan. 4, 2005. U.S. Army Cadet Command. "ROTC Curriculum Review Board: Curriculum Review, Revision and Validation, Creating Flexible Solutions for Developing Warrior Leaders." Fort Monroe, Va.: Cadet Command Leader Development Division. Jan. 4-7, 2005. Thrasher, Maj. Gen. Alan. "Future Force Lieutenant." Fort Monroe, Va.: U.S. Army Cadet Command. July 12, 2004. The objectives listed are a summary of goals and objectives from many presentations held throughout the summer of 2004 to the spring of 2005 dealing with how to create adaptive leaders.

45. At the time of writing, Becker was a first lieutenant. He has just now passed through and graduated from the Special Forces qualification course as an Army captain.

46. The generations of war were covered in detail in the Forward to this monograph, but to reiterate, 1st generation warfare is the era of state warfare, close-quarters fighting proceeding the age of Napoleon. Second generation warfare evolved from the French Revolution, state-versus-state warfare with an emphasis on mobilizing resources to fight centrally-controlled opponents. Third generation warfare evolved from the German attempts during World War II to break the trench stalemate on the Eastern Front by using ideas instead of technology, which prompted the use of decentralized tactics. Finally, 4th generation warfare, of which insurgency is just one aspect, aims to defeat the minds of the opponents' decision-makers through any means possible.

47. Packer, George. "The Next War." The New Yorker. September 2004.

48. Ibid. In addition, I would like to thank 1st Lts. Jordan Becker and Patrick Fagan for their insights into my work and how junior officers adapted, and did not adapt, in Iraq.

49. Cahlink, George. "Trial by Fire." Government Executive Magazine. Washington, D.C.: National Journal Group. April 2005. pp. 52-59.

50. I must thank the former professor of military science at Georgetown University, Lt. Col. Bridgett McCullough for her support of my efforts as well as her efforts to start the ROTC program at Georgetown down the road toward excellence. When she retired, I was fortunate to have the continued support of Lt. Col. Allen Gill, who continued to fine-tune the reforms he observed during Jordan's last year. McCullough and I both arrived in the summer of 1999, when Becker was then a junior (MS III). I got to spend my first two years observing Jordan's last two years as a MS III and senior (MS IV). The last half of Jordan's senior year, during the spring of 2001, was when McCullough made me the Military Science III (junior) instructor, and I began to implement my ideas based on a year and half of observations, and experience from one year serving as the MS III instructor at Duke University Army ROTC under the great leadership and support of Lt. Col. Bill Adams. I was also Jordan's Ranger Challenge team coach his senior year, and we spent a lot of time before and after training talking about how cadets should be prepared to be officers. I also need to thank McCullough for placing Sgt. 1st Class Jeffery Roper with me as a partner in teaching the MS IIIs. Jeff was an extraordinary leader and light infantryman. I was fortunate to have him as a teaching partner and as a friend. He also allowed me to bounce and refine many of my concepts off of him from 2001 to the spring of 2003 (he left Georgetown University ROTC in September 2003).

51. Cahlink, George, "Trial by Fire," pp. 58-59.

52. Survey provided by Jordan Becker to author, Feb. 17, 2005. Also cited in Cahlink, George, "Trial by Fire," p. 59.

53. Another period of major reform happened after the Vietnam War. In my book, Path to Victory: America's Army and the Revolution in Human Affairs, I discuss this period in chapter 5, "Renaissance of the 1980s." While dramatic, the changes here did not evolve beyond 2nd generation warfare, which was designed to fight the Soviets on the North German Plain.

54. The 17 focus areas include: (1) the soldier; (2) force stabilization; (3) joint expeditionary army with a campaign-quality capability (formerly called joint and expeditionary mindset); (4) the bench; (5) combat training centers/Battle Command Training Program; (6) leader development and education; (7) current to future force; (8) Army aviation; (9) modularity; (10) the network; (11) active component/reserve component balance; (12) installations as flagships; (13) actionable intelligence; (14) authorities, responsibilities and accountability; (15) resource processes; (16) strategic communications; and (17) logistics. To view a synopsis of each area, visit: http://www.army.mil/thewayahead/focus.

55. Fastabend and Simpson.

56. At the time of writing, Gen. Kevin Byrnes was the TRADOC commander, in which the author was in communication with referencing his "Raising the Bar" study from March through May 2005. Gen. William Wallace became the new TRADOC commander in October 2005, and has also set TRADOC on a bold path to reform leader development.

57. Byrnes, Gen. Kevin. "State of TRADOC." Speech given to the Association of the United States Army Breakfast, March 3, 2005, in Crystal City, Va. I was also fortunate to meet and talk to Byrnes about the concept of Basic Officer Leadership Course (BOLC) prior to his speech, and then I attended the speech and was pleased to hear a general, and a four-star general at that, proclaim the Army was not good at something – "the mental development of our leaders" – and recommend a fix.

58. Department of the Army. "TRADOC Pam 525-3-0, The Army in Joint Operations; The Army's Future Force Capstone Concept, 2015-2024." Fort Monroe, Va.: U.S. Army Training and Doctrine Command. April 2005.

59. This point was made by a prominent journalist who has been to Iraq numerous times after reading and viewing the Army response to Dr. Leonard Wong's manuscript: "Developing Adaptive Leaders: The Crucible Experience of Operation Iraqi Freedom." Strategic Studies Institute. Carlisle, Penn.: U.S. Army War College. July 2004.

60. Stewart, S. R. "Correlates of Problem Solving and an Evaluation of Training to Increase Problem Solving Effectiveness." Unpublished doctoral dissertation. Carbondale: Southern Illinois University, 1989.

61 . Tillson, J., et al. "Learning to Adapt to Asymmetric Threats." Institute for Defense Analyses. August 2005. p. 19.

62. Discussions with Steven Stewart, March 14, 2005.

63. Based on discussions, both face to face and through e-mails, with Col. George Reed, director of leadership development for the U.S. Army War College, February through April 2005.

64. Deming, W. Edwards. Out of the Crisis. Cambridge: MIT Press. 1986.

65. Clark, Don. Discussion found on "About a Little Dog and Big Dog's Bowl's of Biscuits." A blog about management and leadership. Accessed on April 10, 2005, at http://www.nwlink.com/~donclark/index. html.

66. Accessed on April 10, 2005, at http://www.armystudyguide.com/leadership/studyguide.htm.

67. Jones, Col. Steven. "Raising the Ante on Building Teams." Military Review. Fort Leavenworth, Kan.: U.S. Army Command and General Staff College. July-August 2004. p. 4.

68. Ibid.

69. Sper, David. ed. What does God Expect of a Man? Grand Rapids, Mich.: RBC Ministries. 1989. Accessed on April 10, 2005, at http://www.rbc.org/ds/q0504/point4.html.

70. Discussions with William S. Lind, December 2004.

71. See: http://www.google.com/search?hl=en&lr=&oi=defmore&q=define:Adaptability.

72. Tillson, et al., "Learning to Adapt to Asymmetric Threats," p. 9.

73. Much of the training in pre-commissioning courses, the Officer Basic Course, the Basic Noncommissioned Officer Course, the Officer Advanced Course, CAS3, the Advanced Noncommissioned Officer Course, the Command and General Staff College, the Sergeants Major Academy, and to a lesser degree the School for Advanced Military Studies all teach the MDMP as the core to decision-making; they structure much of their course instruction around the process. Author's observation made through attendance to most of these schools and through discussion with people who attended the others.

74. For more of the history behind this evolution and an understanding of why the U.S. Army went this way, see http://www.d-n-i.net/vandergriff/rha/index.htm; see also Vandergriff, Path to Victory: America's Army and the Revolution in Human Affairs, 2002.

75. The observation-orientation-decision-action (OODA) loop is also known as the Boyd Cycle. It was developed by the late Col. John Boyd based on his observations of jet fighter combat over Korea, and then through years of intense study of why humans react the way they do, or why they make certain decisions in combat. The OODA loop uses the cognitive skills that quantify the situational decision-making process in tangible terms. It transitions decision-making theory into a simplistic and useful approach to teach and improve decision-making.

76. I have been very fortunate to have been mentored by many of the acolytes of John Boyd, particularly Franklin "Chuck" Spinney and Chester Richards. Also see www.d-n-i.net for a thorough examination of Boyd's theories.

77. Wong, Leonard. "Developing Adaptive Leaders: The Crucible Experience of Operation Iraqi Freedom."

78. Ibid.

79. Discussions with Leonard Wong and Col. George Reed, director of leadership development for the Army War College, April 14, 2005.

80. This is based on discussions with Sgt. Maj. Jackson, command sergeant major of the 3rd ROTC Brigade, and Lt. Col. Allen Gill on April 2, 2005. Recent investigations and court-martials show that the responsibility for misconduct has been placed increasingly on the shoulders of lower ranking non-commissioned officers and soldiers. A code in the officer corps has been that a commander is responsible for everything their unit does or does not do.

81. Both journalists asked not to be named, but both returned from Iraq in the fall of 2004, and have made multiple trips to Iraq and Afghanistan.

82. Beck, Sgt. Maj. Rodney L. "The Platoon Sergeant and the Lieutenant: Who does What?" Field Artillery Journal. Fort Sill, Okla.: The Field Artillery School Press. Fall 2001. According to Beck, "The Army does a great job of teaching NCOs how to train soldiers, but a poor job of teaching NCOs how to train and develop their young officers."

83. Peters, Lt. Col. Ralph. "A Grave New World: 10 lessons from the war in Iraq." Armed Forces Journal. Springfield, Va.: Defense News Media Group. April 2005. p. 34.

84. Formal Survey with Capt. Paul Wilcox, Jan. 29, 2005.

85. Reed, Col. George. "Toxic Leaders." Military Review. Fort Leavenworth, Kan.: U.S. Army Command and General Staff College. July-August 2004. pp. 68-69.

86. Ibid.

87. Taguba, Maj. Gen. Antonio M. "Executive Summary of Article 15-6 Investigation of the 800th Military Police Brigade." Available at http://www.msnbc.msn.com/id/4894001/. The report disclosed the large number of officers that were incompetent at their assigned duties, as well as those who displayed the traits of poor leadership.

88. I received similar responses talking to several fellow officers about the Abu Ghraib scandal and I asked, "Where were those soldiers' leaders while this was going on?"

89. Author interview with 1st Lt. Patrick Fagan, October 2004.

90. Dillon, Kathleen A. "Manning the Army After Next (AAN) Force: Critical Examination of the Officer Accession System." Strategy Research Project. Carlisle, Penn.: U.S. Army War College. April 7, 1999.

91 . Cohen, Eliot. "The Future of the United States Army." Speech at American Enterprise Institute symposium. Washington, D.C. April 11, 2005.

92. This essentially explains the bold attempts to move to stabilization policies. These policies created the intangible benefits seen in spring 2005 with high reenlistment rates among those divisions that move to and from the theater of operation as a unit. Soldiers reenlisted for their comrades and unit families, which appeared to be omitted by the press as to the reason soldiers reenlisted.

93. Discussions with Maj. Ike Wilson, December 2004 to January 2005.

94. Stabb, L. Transforming Army Leadership: The Key to Officer Retention. Strategic Research Project, Carlisle, Penn.: U.S. Army War College. 2001. p. 17.

95. Ulmer, Walter. "Creating and Assessing Productive Organizational Climates." Army War College Course Handout. Carlisle, Penn.: U.S. Army War College. 2002. p. 1.

96. Franklin "Chuck" Spinney is an acolyte of the late and famous Col. John Boyd, who developed theories of war, particularly the observe-orient-decide-action cycle so widely known today. Chuck focused his work on reforming the budgetary and weapons procurement processes, but he also wrote extensively on war. When he retired he was honored by a one-hour show on the Jim Lehrer News Hour about his efforts.

97. U.S. Army Field Manual (FM) 22-100. Army Leadership. Washington, D.C.: U.S. Government Printing Office. 1999.

98. "Army Campaign Plan." Available from the Army home page at http://www.army.mil.

99. Gray, Colin. Keynote speech, U.S. Army 16th Annual Strategy Conference. Carlisle, Penn.: U.S. Army War College. April 13, 2005. According to Gray, "Although the National Defense Strategy states 'we are a nation at war,' not many Americans (nor our allies) feel they are at war. Strategic thinking has been an endangered activity in the U.S. for some time. Most officials don't know what it is or how it works."

Center for American Progress. "The Draft: Inevitable, Avoidable or Preferable?" Mark Shields, moderator, Washington, D.C., March 30, 2005. Shields asked at the conference, "I mean, did George Bush know what he was doing when he didn't ask us to sacrifice? First war in 145 years that we've gone to without a draft and with three tax cuts – patriotism light. You put a sticker on your SUV, and that just shows, boy, I'm with the troops. I mean, war demands equality of sacrifice."

100. Just a note to keep in mind: if it somehow confuses the reader as they begin to think of what reform is going to mean in this chapter, it is not going to imply "touchy feely" ideas, or make it easier, or for that matter imply a "return to the good old days." As a matter of fact, the recommendations made herein seek to achieve professionalism, thus raising the standards of entrance.

101. Discussions with Lt. Col. Allen Gill, professor of military science at Georgetown University, October 2003-November 2004; Shinseki chose not to make the personnel system part of transformation due to his concern that that would be taking on too much under his watch. To his credit, however, he did allow for the beginning of studies to begin under the Unit Manning Task Force in September 2002. Also, the author was part of the Unit Manning Task force sanctioned by Gen. Jack Keane, vice chief of staff of the Army. In addition, author brief to Gen. John Keane, Army vice chief of staff, June 17, 2002. I credit Shinseki with beginning transformation, and also admire his moral courage.

102. The author attended a symposium on the transformation of the reserve components held at Georgetown University in September 2004. I happened to walk in on a panel discussion where the subject of reforming the personnel system came up from the audience! Several members of the panel had, of course, in the past disagreed with the proposals made in Path to Victory, and in many of my briefings to senior leaders and politicians. One audience member, who had written a scathing review of Path to Victory two years prior, made public proclamations that the personnel system had to be changed before effective reform of the military and reserves could be implemented.

103. Lang, Kurt. "Military Organizations." Handbook of Organizations. ed. James G. March. Chicago: Rand McNally & Co. 1965. pp. 843-857.

104. Tillson, John. "Reducing the Impact of Tempo." Institute for Defense Analyses. Alexandria, Va.: IDA Press. October 1999. pp. 57-68.

105. Naylor, Sean. "It's the Personnel System, Stupid: Secretary White's fast track push to reform on how the Army mans its units." Army Times. Springfield, Va.: Army Times Publishing. Sept. 14, 2002. These words were actually taken from one of my briefings, "The People Side of Transformation," which I provided to White and his speechwriter, Col. Nick Nicholson.

106. Vandergriff, Donald E. "The Revolution of Human Affairs." Available at http://www.d-n-i.net/vandergriff/rha/sld039.htm.

107. Ulmer, Col. Walt. and Malone, Col. Mike. Study of Professionalism. Carlisle, Penn.: U.S. Army War College. June 30, 1970. p. 22.

108. Ibid. p. iv.

109. In 1970, Lt. Gen. William F. Peers sent Army Chief of Staff Gen. William C. Westmoreland a memo in which he reported that officers were shirking responsibility, lying, turning a blind eye to improper conduct, commanding from a safe distance, ignoring their men's concerns and failing to enforce measures to protect their troops. The effects of such behavior on soldiers' ability to manage the stresses of combat have been documented in extensive post-traumatic stress disorder (PTSD) literature and the collapse of discipline in the Army. Some soldiers in the field, exasperated by certain officers' self-seeking behavior and indifference to their subordinates' welfare, tried to kill them (often referred to as "fragging") – sometimes successfully. To his credit, Westmoreland tasked the U.S. Army War College to look into the Army's leadership climate.

110. Ibid. pp. vi-ix.

111. Vandergriff. Path to Victory, pp. 107-118.

112. Ibid. pp. 108-109.

113. Ibid. pp. 181-184, 263-4 and 271. It must be noted that the Army moved through OPMS XXI in order to move officers to other fields and to give fewer officers more time in those battalion line jobs (now the length of time in battalion line jobs has been extended from one year to almost three years).

114. TTHS accounts for those soldiers – officers and enlisted – that are in transition or not currently serving with a unit or a temporary duty unit (TDY). At any one time, 60,000 to 70,000 soldiers belong to this account. The account is driven by the individual replacement system (IRS) and policies that branch off the up-or-out promotion system.

115. For a more detailed argument, see: Bondy, Harry J. "Postmodernism and the Source of Military Strength in the Anglo West." Armed Forces & Society. College Park, Md. November 2004. Vol. 31, Issue 1.

116. Jones, Col. Stephen. "Improving Accountability for Effective Command Climate: A Strategic Imperative." Strategic Studies Institute. Carlisle, Penn.: U.S. Army War College. September 2003. p. v.117 For the best two descriptions of the Prussian/German officer accessions process see: Gudmundsson, Bruce I. Stormtroop Tactics: German Innovation 1914-1918. New York: Praeger. 1995. Corum, James. Roots of Blitzkrieg. Lawrence, Kan.: University Press of Kansas, 2000. For a good summary, see http://www.d-n-i.net/vandergriff/rha/sld034.htm and slide 35.

118. Bondy, Lt. Col. Harry J. "New Regiments, New Specialist Corps, and a New General Staff." Journal of Military and Strategic Studies. Canadian Defense and Foreign Affairs Institute. Winter 2004. pp. 3-5.

119. Wilson, III, Maj. Isaiah. "Educating the Post-Modern U.S. Army Strategic Planner: Improving the Organizational Construct." Fort Leavenworth, Kan.: U.S. Army School of Advanced Military Studies. February 2003. pp. 43-44.

120. Author e-mail correspondence with Lt. Col. Harry J. Bondy (Canadian Army), April 2005. Also see: Bondy, "New Regiments, New Specialist Corps, and A New General Staff." pp. 3-5. Available at http://www.jmss.org/2004/winter/articlesbody5.htm. Bondy and the author have shared many facts and ideas over the last few years. Many of the factors that affect the U.S. Army also affect the Canadian Army.

121. Bondy, "New Regiments, New Specialist Corps, and A New General Staff," p. 3.

122. Spinney, Franklin C. and Sayen, Lt. Col. John. "Sayen Report: Officer Bloat Creates a Shortage of Captains," Defense and National Interest. July 16, 2000. Accessed at http://www.d-n-i.net/fcs/comments/ c372.htm.

123. Bell, William. "The Impact of Policies on Organizational Values and Culture." Paper presented at the Joint Services Conference on Professional Ethics. January 1999.

124. Snider, D. M. And G.L. Watkins (2000). "The Future of Army Professionalism: A Need for Renewal and Redefinition." Parameters. Vol. 30, Issue 3. pp. 5-20.

125. Mason, Ensign Steven. "Positive and Negative Leadership Models." Published at www.d-n-i.net. May 20, 2004. Available at http://www.d-n-i.net/fcs/pdf/boydleadership.pdf. This study provides an innovative application of Boyd's organizational climate to leadership at all levels. Also in reference to author's discussions with Dr. Steven Stewart, John Tillson and cadets of the Georgetown ROTC Program, particularly cadets with prior service in the Army.

126. "Secretary of Defense 2003 Summer Study: The Military Officer in 2030." Unpublished briefing. Washington, D.C.: Department of Defense, Office of Net Assessment. Summer 2003. p. 41. Author's note: I was not invited to the actual conference held at the Naval War College, but I was asked to attend the out-briefings in the fall of 2003 and 2002.

127. Kotter references this in his commentary on eight errors an organization makes when trying to change, such as declaring victory too early.

128. Shay, Jonathan. Achilles in Vietnam. United Kingdom: Scribner. 1995.

129. Argysis, Chris. "Making the Undiscussable and Its Undiscussability Discussable." Public Administration Review. Boston, Mass.: American Society for Public Administration. May-June 1980. pp. 205-213.

130. E-mail correspondence with Col. Chris Paparone, former instructor on leadership, U.S. Army War College.

131. Wilcox, Lt. Col. Greg. "Information Operations and 4GW." SRI International. Arlington, Va.: SRI International Press. Feb. 23, 2005.

132. Discussions with Maj. Isaiah Wilson, December 2004 through April 2005.

133. Ibid.

134. "Company Command – Building Combat-Ready Teams: Reflexive Fire Training – Taking Marksmanship to a New Level." Army. Arlington, Va.: Association of the United States Army. May 2005. p. 13. Available at www.companycommand.army.mil and http://www.ausa.org. May 2, 2005.

135. Baxin, Capt. Aaron A. "Boyd's O-O-D-A Loop and the Infantry Company Commander." Infantry. Fort Benning, Ga.: U.S. Army Infantry Association, January-February 2005. p. 17.

136. Ibid. p. 17.

137. Ibid, p. 17.

138. Ibid. p. 19.

139. Mackey, Col. Richard H., Sr. "Translating Vision into Reality: The Role of the Strategic Leader." Student Study Project. Carlisle Barracks, Penn.: U.S. Army War College, 1992. Schein, Edgar H. Organizational Culture and Leadership. San Francisco, Calif.: Jossey-Bass, 1992. Setear, John K., Builder, Carl H., Baccus, M. D., and Madewell, Wayne. The Army in a Changing World: The Role of Organizational Vision. Santa Monica, Calif.: Rand Corp. 1990. Snider, Don M. "The National Security Strategy: Documenting Strategic Vision." Strategic Studies Institute. Carlisle Barracks, Penn.: U.S. Army War College. February 1992.

140. Kotter, John P. "Winning at Change." Leader to Leader. Vol. 10. Fall 1998. pp. 27-33.

141. Brownlee, Les and Gen. Schoomaker, Peter. "Serving a Nation at War: Toward a Campaign Quality Army with Joint and Expeditionary Qualities." Parameters. The Army War College. Carlisle, Penn. p.18.

142. A prevalent complaint from competent leaders – officers and NCOs – that I gathered through my interviews and from the surveys I administrated 2004-2005 was the varied quality of the officer corps. Accompanying this issue, was the concern by these leaders on the ethical conduct of the cadre who ran and allowed these people to get commissioned.

143. Mason, Ensign Steven. "Positive and Negative Leadership Models," and author discussions with Col. Chet Richards and Ensign Steve Mason.

144. Killebrew, Col. Robert B., U.S. Army (Ret.). "Toward an Adaptive Army." Army Magazine. September 2002.

145. Schoomaker, Gen. Peter. "The Future of the United States Army." Remarks given at the American Enterprise Symposium. "The Future of the United States Army." April 11, 2005.

146. Schmitt, John F. "Command and (Out of) Control: The Military Implications of Complexity Theory."

147. Ibid. p. 5.

148. Ibid. p. 5.

149. Ibid. p. 6.

150. U.S. Army. "Warrior Ethos Task Force: CSA Outbrief." May 23, 2003.

151. Fastabend and Simpson.

152. Fastabend and Simpson.

153. E-mail discussions with Bruce I. Gudmundsson, Dec. 16, 2004. Gudmundsson noted, "Put another way, it is no accident that Pestalozzi focused on 'pre-school' – the education of very young children – and that many German officers referred to TDGs as 'pre-school' ['Vorschule'] for tactics." For information on Pestalozzi,   see http://www.cals.ncsu.edu/agexed/aee501/pestalozzi.html.

154. Ibid.

155. Schmitt, Maj. John F. "The How To of Tactical Decision Games." Marine Corps University Publications. Quantico, Va. 1994.

156. Brownlee, Les and Schoomaker, Gen. Peter. "Serving a Nation at War: Toward a Campaign Quality Army with Joint and Expeditionary Qualities," Parameters. The Army War College. Carlisle, Penn. 2004. p. 19.

157. Gatto, John Taylor. "The Prussian Connection." The Underground History of American Education: An Intimate Investigation into the Problem of Modern Schooling. New York: New Society Publishers. 1991. p. 79.

158. Records and notes of Sgt. 1st Class Jeff Roper and Maj. Don Vandergriff. September 2000 to September 2003.159. This comment came from briefing a colonel at Cadet Command on "Raising the Bar," and this was his initial reaction. As the briefing went on, he realized that the stress of ACM exposes students of weaker character faster than the proficiency focused training. Thus, the signs of weak ethical conduct could be dealt with earlier than later, when it may cost a unit and its soldiers in lives.

160. Records and notes of Sgt. 1st Class Jeff Roper and Maj. Don Vandergriff. September 2000 to September 2003.

161. Ibid.

162. As of June 2005, the Army is already taking preliminary steps in defining the importance of teaching in its quest to become adaptive. Schoomaker has directed the designation of a Military Occupancy Skill identifier for teachers.

163. Skelton, Ike. "JPME: Are We There Yet?" Military Review. May 1992. p. 2.

164. Author interview with Capt. Paul Wilcox, June 2005. Wilcox got his wish. He commanded a tank and headquarters and headquarters company in the 4th Infantry Division in Iraq and at Fort Hood, then became a platoon TAC at the Army's new Basic Officer Leader Course (BOLC) II at Fort Benning, Ga., where he is slated to assume command of one of the BOLC II training companies as his third command.

165. Six cohorts (years) of cadets from Georgetown University reflect on how well they were prepared to make decisions in combat, in contrast to their peers from other ROTC programs, as well as USMA and OCS.

166. http://en.wikipedia.org/wiki/Jedi_Knight#Origins_of_the_Order. It is Japanese for "period drama" movies about samurai. Also see, Wass de Czege, Brig. Gen. Huba. Army Staff College Level Training Study. Carlisle Barracks, Penn. U.S. Army War College. 1983. This was also a label placed on the graduates of the Army's elite School of Advanced Military Studies created by Wass de Czege in 1981-1982 and began in 1983.

167. Moilanen, Jon. "Leader Competency and Army Readiness." Military Review. Vol. 82. July-August 2002. p. 62.

168. Ibid. p. 78.

169. Discussions with Col. Robert Frusha, commander of the Eastern ROTC Region, July 17, 2004. Frusha made many positive changes to the ROTC leader's training course, which was once considered a gentleman's course or summer camp. The leader's training course is held between sophomore and junior years of ROTC, and also allows many programs to laterally transfer cadets into their programs without the cadet having to progress through the Military Science I and II years.

170. Morsy, Zaghloul (ed.). Thinkers on Education. pp. 21-45.

171. This was also referred to as "deliberate practice" in Ross, K. and Lussier, J.W. "Adaptive Thinking Seminar." Arlington, Va.: Army Research Institute. 2000.

172. LePine, J.A. Colquitt and Erez, A. "Adaptability to Changing Task Contexts: Effects of general cognitive ability, conscientiousness, and openness to experience." Personnel Psychology. 2000. pp. 563-593.

173. Klein, Gary. "The Recognition-Primed Decision (RPD) Model: Looking back, looking forward," Naturalistic Decision Making. ed. C. Zsambok and G. Klein. Mahwah, NJ: Erlbaum. 1997. pp. 285-292.

174. Discussions with Col. Robert Frusha, commander of the Eastern ROTC Region, July 17, 2004.

175. Gatto, John Taylor. "The Prussian Connection."

176. Vandergriff, Donald E., "Lessons Learned with Decision Making."

177. See e-mail discussions with Bruce I. Gudmundsson, Dec. 16, 2004, on the use of tactical decision games (TDGs). Bruce added, "It is not so much "training" and "pre-training." That is to say, they serve to develop habits that are conducive to the use of all sorts of other methods, to include more elaborate simulations and field exercises, to study tactics."

178. Klein, Gary. The Power of Intuition: How to Use Your Gut Feelings to Make Better Decisions. New York: Currency. 2003.

179. Our cadre downloaded Marine Corps Gazette archived TDGs, converted Marine to Army language and modified them further to teach the adaptability principle of that period.

180. Phillips, Jennifer; McCloskey, Michael; McDermott, Patricia; Wiggins, Sterling; Battaglia, Deborah; Thordsen, Marving; and Klein, Gary. "Decision-Centered MOUT Training for Small Unit Leaders." Arlington, Va.: Army Research Institute (ARI). August 2001. p. 20.

181. Schmitt, John F. Mastering Tactics. Quantico, Va.: U.S. Marine Corps Association. 1994. p. 3.

182. The Marine Corps Gazette TDG website, http://www.mca-marines.org/Gazette/tdg.htm, also archives past TDGs with solutions.

183. See http://lafdtraining.org/tdg. Also see http://www.usachcs.army.mil/TACarchive/ACwinspro3/Edwards.htm.

184. Conversations with Maj. Philip Peck, March through June 2005. He has eight scenarios available.

185. Kilpatrick, William H. "Introduction to Heinrich Pestalozzi." The Education of Man – Aphorisms. New York: Philosophical Library. 1951.

186. Vandergriff, Donald E., "Lessons Learned with Decision Making."

187. Ibid.

188. While at Georgetown Army ROTC, I found computer based war-games were another good tool for building adaptability; however students had to be reminded how the games compare to reality. It is easy to play the game in the comfort of one's dorm room, in the dead of winter, or heat of summer with no other restrictions or stress. One way to determine evolutionary adaptability is having several students play the same virtual game scenario with time restrictions, and then view how far they got or whether any of the students solved the scenario. Also, how many times did it take the students to play the same scenario to solve it? Most war games alter the play of the artificial intelligence every time a scenario is repeated.

189. Vandergriff, Donald E., "Lessons Learned with Decision Making."

190. Ulmer, Walter. "Notes on Leadership for the 1980s." Military Review. Reprint from July 1980. January-February 1997. p. 77.

191. Ulmer, Walter. "Creating and Assessing Productive Organizational Climates." Army War College Course Handout. Carlisle, Penn.: U.S. Army War College. 2002. p. 1.

192. Brewster, Maj. Frank. "Using Tactical Decision Exercises to Study Tactics." Military Review. November-December 2002. p. 3.

193. Fastabend and Simson, p. 6

194. Discussion with Steven Stewart, March 2005.

195. Fastabend and Simson, p. 6

Acronyms

1GW   First Generation Warfare
2GW   Second Generation Warfare
3GW   Third Generation Warfare
4GW   Fourth Generation Warfare
AAR   After Action Review
ACC   Army Cadet Command
ACM   Adaptive Course Model
AIT   Advanced Individual Training
ARI   Army Research Institute
BOLC   Basic Officer Leadership Course
BT   Basic Training
C&GSC   U.S. Army Command and General Staff College
COE   Current Operating Environment
CTC   Combat Training Center
DMG   Decision Making Games
FCS   Future Combat System
FRAGO   Fragmentary Orders
GFE   Graded Field Evaluations
GWOT   Global War on Terror
HUMINT   Human Intelligence
IED   Improvised Explosive Device
JRTC   Joint Readiness Training Center
LEA   Leadership Evaluation Approach
LDE   Leadership Development Exercises
MDMP   Military Decision-Making Process
MILES   Military Laser Simulation of Real Bullets
MILPERCEN   Military Personnel Center
MOUT   Military Operations in Urban Terrain
MRE   Meal Ready to Eat
NCO   Non-Commissioned Officer
NTC   National Training Center
OBC   Officer Basic Course
OER   Officer Evaluation Report
OES   Officer Education System
OODA   Observation Orientation Decision Action

OPA   Officer Personnel Act
OPMS Officer Personnel Management System
OPORD   Operation Order
PME   Professional Military Education
POI   Programs of Instruction
ROTC   Reserve Officer Training Corps
SAMS   School of Advanced Military Studies
TA   Teacher of Adaptability
TBE   Terrain Board Exercise
TDG   Tactical Decision Games
TRADOC Training and Doctrine Command
TTHS   The Training Hospital and School
XO   Executive Officer

Made in the USA
Monee, IL
21 February 2021